CONTACTING

YOUR

SPIRIT GUIDE

ALSO BY SYLVIA BROWNE

Books/Card Decks

Accepting the Psychic Torch

Adventures of a Psychic (with Antoinette May)

Animals on the Other Side (with Chris Dufresne)

Astrology Through a Psychic's Eyes

Blessings from the Other Side (with Lindsay Harrison)

Christmas in Heaven

Conversations with the Other Side

Exploring the Levels of Creation

Father God

God, Creation, and Tools for Life

Heart and Soul card deck

If You Could See What I See

Insight (with Lindsay Harrison)

A Journal of Love and Healing
(with Nancy Dufresne)

Life on the Other Side (with Lindsay Harrison)

Meditations

Mother God

My Psychic Journey (with Chris Dufresne)

Mystical Traveler

The Mystical Life of Jesus

THE JOURNEY OF THE SOUL SERIES
(available individually or in a boxed set)

Audio/CD Programs

SYLVIA BROWNE

Contacting

— YOUR —

Spirit Guide

DISCOVER MESSAGES, HELP, AND HEALING FROM THE OTHER SIDE

HAY HOUSE, INC.
Carlsbad, California • New York City
London • Sydney • New Delhi

Library of Congress Control Number for the Original Edition:
2004116381

Tradepaper ISBN: 978-1-4019-6583-9
E-book ISBN: 978-1-4019-1948-1

10 9 8 7 6 5 4 3 2
1st edition, December 2002
2nd edition, September 2005
3rd edition, January 2015
4th edition, October 2021

Printed in the United States of America

To Francine and Raheim . . . without them,
this book would not have been possible.
And to Dal Brown . . . who has been such
an aid in editing and encouragement.

CONTENTS

BONUS CONTENT

Thank you for purchasing *Contacting Your Spirit Guide* by Sylvia Browne. This product includes a free download of "Spirit Guide Meditation"! To access this bonus content, please visit www.hayhouse.com/download and enter the Product ID and Download Code as they appear below.

Product ID: 2490
Download Code: ebook

For further assistance, please contact Hay House Customer Care by phone: US (800) 654-5126 or INTL CC+(760) 431-7695 or visit www.hayhouse.com/contact.php.

Thank you again for your Hay House purchase. Enjoy!

CONTACTING YOUR SPIRIT GUIDE
AUDIO DOWNLOAD TRACK LIST

1. Introduction
2. Spirit Guide Meditation

Caution: This audio program features meditation/visualization exercises that render it inappropriate for use while driving or operating heavy machinery.

Publisher's note: Hay House products are intended to be powerful, inspirational, and life-changing tools for personal growth and healing. They are not intended as a substitute for medical care. Please use this audio program under the supervision of your care provider. Neither the author nor Hay House, Inc. assumes any responsibility for your improper use of this product.

INTRODUCTION

I usually start out my books by talking about how many years of research have gone into the particular work. While it's true that much research has been done in the preparation of *this* book, it's different from the others in a sense. The reason is that it encompasses a personal story that's very close to my heart—one that details not just the reality of spirit guides, but the very real odyssey of my life with my primary guide, Francine, who's been with me since the very beginning of my journey in this lifetime. She and I made a pact, as we all do before we come into life, that she'd be helping me along the way. In turn, she and I would both "learn" for God and complete our mission in life.

We write our life's chart with the help of a group of friends, helpers, and the "Council," which is comprised of wise "master teachers," all of whom help us map out our purpose. Then the spirit guide comes in to study with us and to help as much as possible. After 68 years of being with *my* guide, Francine, I can truthfully say that she is my dearest, most treasured friend. Have I always agreed with her? Absolutely not! Have I tested her? Definitely. But I have to say that she's usually right, notwithstanding my sometimes stubborn need to argue with her.

I hope that this book gives you an insight into spirit guides—these often silent, omnipresent, patient helpers who have no other agenda but to get us through this life in the best way we can, and then go back Home to God. I had to laugh to myself when I read what well-known medium Arthur Ford's guide (Fletcher) replied when he was asked during a trance session if he would ever like to hold this position again. Fletcher responded without hesitation, "Never!" I'm sure that most guides tend to feel this way.

What people may not realize is that although spirit guides are quite advanced entities who exist on a very high vibrational level, they still have to be somewhat humanized. If they weren't, they really wouldn't give a damn what happens to us. So, of all the entities who reside on the Other Side, I'd say that spirit guides display more human-type emotions than any of them. And I thank God that they do. After all, who'd want a spirit guide who acted like an unfeeling robot—with the attitude that whatever trauma you were experiencing would soon pass and that you'd forget all about it once you returned to the Other Side?

So, if you should ever feel abandoned and alone, I want you to remember that you're never without protection or companionship. Not only is God omnipresent, but so are Jesus, the angels, and last but not least, the often unsung heroes who stand patiently by—loving, helping, and healing us: *our spirit guides*.

PART I
CONTACTING
YOUR
SPIRIT GUIDE

CHAPTER 1

WHAT IS A SPIRIT GUIDE?

Many people are bewildered when it comes to what a spirit guide is. I understand this confusion, because each of us has angels (10 categories in all); our loved ones who have passed before us to the Other Side; and ghosts, who are souls who haven't made it to the Other Side and feel that they're still alive. We also have what can often be hard to discern: energy implants. With an energy implant, there isn't any entity present, but a trauma is implanted by an individual at a particular place and time, and a psychic can then pick up the events imprinted in that soul's energy.

In this book, however, I want to focus on spirit guides. These are entities who have lived life on this earthly plane. They can be male or female, and they're very solid in their own dimension on the Other Side. They study your chart (our program that we choose to

CONTACTING YOUR SPIRIT GUIDE

come into life with) and help you decide the lessons you're here to learn, and also how they can help you do so. To put it in the simplest terms possible, you made a contract with this particular entity to watch over you while you're in life.

Many guides often study for a long time to be your guide so that they can get your chart right. Of course you have help from the Council, too—the spirit guide will approach the Council before your birth and even after you come into life for advice and guidance with their charge (that's *you*).

Sometimes spirit guides have lived lives with you, but this is fairly rare. Guides can't be relatives who died when you were three years old or younger, because that would mean that you went unattended for a period of time. No, the guide is with you when you enter, and it's there throughout your life. The guide even helps to take you to the Other Side, along with your loved ones, angels, and souls you cared about before you came into life, but whom you haven't necessarily known on Earth.

Spirit guides come in all shapes and sizes, and they're from all different cultures. They can assume any visage, but I assure you, they're trusted, valued friends who will never disappoint you. They have great wisdom and courage, and you'll hear from them if you're quiet and listen. Guides don't always have an audible voice, although the more you believe in their existence, the better they're able to communicate.

Maybe I had an edge because I came from a long line of psychics (going back 300 years!)—but I actually heard my guide speak to me when I was seven years old (I'll discuss this in detail later in the book). In the beginning, she didn't give me a running commentary, but she did give me messages. Please understand, this all started 61 years ago, and it was a much different world back then—one where people couldn't even begin to accept this concept—not to mention the fact that I was born into a Catholic/ Jewish/ Episcopalian/ Lutheran household. None of this lent itself to making contact with a disembodied spirit. When people now tell me that they're struggling with similar confusion and fear, I understand completely.

I found out back then that my guide's name was Iena, and how my family and I got Francine out of this is beyond all of our memories. Maybe I just didn't like the name and changed it. Who knows? A guide's name isn't really critical, but I've found that it's significant to at least know what *sex* your guide is and to have some identity basis—if nothing else, it makes them more real to you. I'm also convinced that when we call upon them and believe in them, it helps our guides pierce the veil of the dimensions from the Other Side to this side. (And since this is a question that is often asked, let me clarify: It *is* possible to have more than one guide, as I do—Francine, my primary guide; and Raheim, my secondary guide—but usually you'll have just one.)

To go back to the name issue, I can't tell you how many times I've told people their spirit guides' names, and they've either exclaimed that this has always been their favorite moniker, or that they called their dog that, or their mother was going to give them that very name. It seems that the name of the guide is often imprinted in our consciousness. I've even had people come up with the right name after they "met" their guide during one of the meditative exercises that follows later in this book.

Now, you'll get as many as 20 or 30 messages a day from your guide, but you'll have a tendency to chalk these communications up to your own thoughts, or to coincidence. That doesn't mean that you can't have your own infusion of psychic knowledge from God, but your guide certainly has a voice as well. For example, what made you call Susan and find out if she was sick? What caused you to put on your seat belt the day you had an accident (something you should wear each time you're in a vehicle anyway)? These small and even larger episodes can very well stem from your guide. Unlike angels who protect and heal, your guides, as clairvoyant Ruth Montgomery once said, are "the nudging companions along the way."

CHAPTER 2

HOW SPIRIT GUIDES MAKE THEMSELVES KNOWN

Francine, whom I've received mountains of information from over the years, has always stressed that guides are continually trying to be recognized or accepted so that they can have easier access to us, thereby infusing us with knowledge or telepathically helping us fulfill our chart.

People get aggravated because guides don't always make audible contact, but with patience, you *will* receive their messages, and if you follow the exercises that are presented later on in this book, I'm *convinced* that you will. Let me tell you right now that you won't necessarily hear the voice in the way you expect, though. It's not some soft, ethereal, melodic tone—rather, it's high-pitched and has a fast, almost chipmunk-like sound to it.

My dear friend Lindsay, who has written with me for years, recently heard her spirit guide for the first time. She called me and said, "Sylvia, I heard Rachel, but her voice had a tinny, high-pitched quality."

I replied, "Well, that's just what I've been trying to explain to you all this time!"

In fact, over the years, I've heard the same story from people who've heard this high-pitched voice and want me to clarify what it is. The answer is simple: It's their spirit guide. Francine says that it's hard for guides to manifest and speak, much harder than it is for angels. Not that one phylum (particular sect of beings) is more advanced, per se, but since guides are on a higher, more elevated level, they find it difficult to tune in to the dense atmosphere in which we live. Francine describes it as trying to wade through a thick pea-soup fog.

(Strangely enough, while angels don't audibly verbalize, you can hear them in your mind, although they're not the talkers that the guides are. Also, your deceased loved ones can have a voice that you recognize after they pass over. This is because they were here so recently that they haven't ascended yet, after which it becomes more difficult to communicate. By no means should you feel that you can't hear him or her; it just becomes harder.)

Notwithstanding the fact that an ear infection or sinus drainage on our part may block a guide's ability to communicate, they do give us signals. They can create that hollow, dead-air feeling when external sound disappears for a few moments and the air gets still. They can also create a high-pitched whining sound or popping sensation in your ear.

A friend of mine was just dropping off to sleep when she heard a female voice inside her head clearly say, "My name is Heidi, and I wish you goodnight." She wasn't asleep yet; in fact, she was doing a very visual meditation about spirit guides. My friend sat bolt upright in bed and felt for a few minutes as if she were losing her mind. But that wasn't the case at all—spirit guides will simply use any avenue to make themselves known to us. Francine says that when the person a spirit guide is helping has a breakthrough, the guide experiences what we'd call a sense of jubilation.

Now, the guides are always happy, but since they have to become more humanized in order to be effective in helping us, I can understand why they get even happier when there's a breakthrough. I mean, think about it: What if you were always helping someone but there was never any recognition? It's not that the guides' egos are out of whack—it really helps *you* more than it helps them to acknowledge their existence. The guides are going to do their jobs, regardless. I also feel that it's good that the guides have lived earthly lives, so at least they can have some conscious memory of the pitfalls and tragedies—as well as the joys—that life can bring us.

WHAT DO THE GUIDES LOOK LIKE?

Some guides will appear in what I call their own definitive mode of dress. Some have actually dressed in Roman togas, but they can show up in regular street attire, too. Francine usually appears to me in a flowing chiffon dress, while Raheim tends to wear a white Nehru jacket with a white turban. This doesn't seem to have any particular significance except that it reflects their own individual preference, which proves that we not only keep our own personality on the Other Side, but our taste in dress as well.

Francine began to physically manifest to me when I was 18 years old. When she told me in advance that she would try to do so, my family members quickly took up seats all around the living room. I began to see the folds in her skirt; her long, tapered fingers; her tall, slender form; and a black braid. That was enough, and I closed my eyes. My family watched the full manifestation, but I couldn't. I've often wondered why I wasn't able to, and I've come to the conclusion that I was visionary and auditory enough, and besides, I had to live in this world. (Even though I have psychic ability, I try to stay grounded as much as possible. If you don't, you'll find yourself in this esoteric, "airy-fairy" world where no one can enter except you. This leads to your doing things just for yourself and not for others. Psychic ability is bestowed upon you by God—and it's not supposed to be used for exclusively selfish reasons—it's given to you so that you can assist others.)

But even though I didn't want to see Francine then, she appeared to me anyway. Many years ago when I was living in a low-rent apartment with my kids, I was tucking them in when out of the corner of my eye I saw her in a fully condensed form. She was dressed in this flowing aquamarine dress that seemed to billow out. Her face was oval, with slightly slanted eyes, high cheekbones, and full lips. She smiled and was gone. It was as if she was telling me, "You didn't want to view me earlier, but you'll see me now . . ."

CHAPTER 3

THERE ARE ALL KINDS OF GUIDES

For a while there, it seemed that the popular trend was for everyone who consulted a medium to get the name "Running Water," "Standing Bear," "Silver Fox," or something like that for their guides. Now I'm not trying to dispute the fact that there may be some Native American spirit guides, but it just seems that during my many decades of research, I would have encountered one of them. However, as with everything else, if you do hear a name, roll it around in your mind, see if it feels right, and then use that name—or change it, as I did with Francine. Just do whatever feels comfortable to you. Even though it makes it more personal to call a guide by name, I fully believe that it doesn't matter *what* you call them—as long as you *do* call on them.

Some guides will appear to us as children when we're kids ourselves. My son Christopher, whose guide's name is Charlie, came to him in the form of a little boy and grew up with him. Francine, on the other hand, always seemed to be about 30 years of age and stayed that way. This is somewhat aggravating to me, since I'm now 68 and she's still 30!

I've done enough research to believe that given my childhood (which featured a somewhat absentee mother figure), Francine took on the persona of an older and matriarchal person, while Christopher, who had a strong mother figure (me), might have chosen to have his guide be a helping buddy. In fact, imaginary playmates are spirit guides 99 percent of the time. Guides will come in as children to make it easier for their young charges to learn from them.

Parents should be indulgent and even go so far as to set a place at the table for "Joey," "Sissy," or whomever the playmate may be. If we allow our children to talk freely, they'll not only tell us about their guides, but also about angels and past lives.

When my ministers and I teach Sunday school at our church, the Society of Novus Spiritus, we sometimes hear kids go into long, detailed stories about their guides or angels when we tell them that God always has someone watching over them. Their faces light up, and the words just tumble out.

This sometimes brings back a memory of when I was in the first grade, and the nuns at my school had flip charts that showed saints and angels. I remember raising my hand and saying, "I already know about them; I *hear* mine." I was promptly told to stay after school.

My teacher, Sister Stephanie, told me to never voice that type of thing again. Even as a child, I can remember thinking so vividly, *If you tell us they're there, and I tell you I know it, then why am I in trouble?* My grandmother got wind of this and was up to see the nun the very next day. I don't know what Grandma said to her, but I was never disciplined about this again. Of course, the reason might be that after that incident, I kept quiet in class and only confided in a select few. As my oldest girlfriend, Mary Margaret, once said when asked what it was like to grow up with me, "We'd stand around on the playground and ask Sylvia what was going to happen, and it did!"

I'm very sympathetic when my clients tell me that they have a belief in God, angels, spirit guides, and an afterlife, but their families or spouses do not. Be patient with them. Everyone comes upon their own truth at their own time, and it doesn't help to shove it down anyone's throat, no matter how close they are to you. I always tell my clients to try to have their spirit guide give their loved one a validation. If a guide doesn't do that, then I advise them to believe quietly, in their own way, and not try to convert anyone.

It's amazing to me, though, that through my research into both recent and ancient writings, biblical or otherwise, I've learned that in every religion, without exception, followers believed in prophecy, the concept of a third eye, and in the foretelling of the future; as well as messengers, angels, warning voices, and so on. It seems that the more technologically advanced and capitalistic we've become, the more we've lost our innate ability to get in touch with ourselves, as well as with the Other Side. Like "E.T.," we want to phone Home, but we seem to have lost the number.

CHAPTER 4

DO GUIDES GIVE OUT PSYCHIC INFORMATION?

Spirit guides can help you with your chart, your lessons, and your life in general, but their purpose is not to infuse you with psychic abilities. That gift comes from God, and it's your vehicle through which the record of your life (and others' lives) can be accessed. Can a guide tell your future? Yes . . . if he or she is standing right there reading your chart. But when *you're* attempting to be precognitive, it should be between you and God. That's why even though I hear what Francine has to say, I also ask God before I go to sleep to talk to me or infuse me with knowledge so that I do the right thing and stay on my chart.

In addition, throughout all my years of research—not only with my own clients, but through the study of other mediums such as Edgar Cayce, Margaret Leonard, Douglas Johnson, Arthur Ford, and others—not one of them, including myself, can honestly say that we've gotten much verbal psychic help *for ourselves*. The guides seem to be virtual fountains of knowledge for others, but not for us.

Spirit guides don't give us mediums Lotto numbers or great insights into our future. Certainly guides will nudge us and give us some advice, and they talk to the Council and help us behind the scenes with different situations, but as far as giving us personal, hard-core data—never! Now, Francine *will* give me information about Novus Spiritus and pass on spiritual knowledge, which helps, and she'll also answer specific personal questions in trance sessions for those who ask her . . . but not for me.

It's almost as if mediums are in a tube that allows information to come in for everyone else, but not for us. If you consider this concept further, it makes sense, because if spirit guides verbally instructed us every step of the way, we'd never make mistakes—and therefore, we'd never learn. If I do encounter anyone who gets specific day-to-day guidance, I'm suspicious, because life doesn't work that way. What would be the purpose of coming down to this earthly plane if everything always went perfectly? Mediums have to take their knocks just like everyone else.

Over the years, my friends and ministers have laughed about this situation, and it has become a standing joke, because no matter what happens, Francine's statement to me is, "Everything will be all right." Years ago, out of sheer exasperation, I screamed, "Of course it will! I'll eventually die someday, too, and then everything will definitely be all right!"

I don't want to give the impression that Francine hasn't been right on the mark about some very important milestones in my life, it's just that, like so many of us, I didn't listen. For example, several months before my first marriage, she asked me, "Are you sure you want to do this?" You'd think that this would have been enough of a clue to me, but no, I had to have it my way. She also told me years ago that I'd have two boys and would end up living in California. So, while there are definite bullet points, what I'm trying to convey here is that the day-to-day verbal guidance that people may expect . . . well, it doesn't happen. Daily occurrences are, nevertheless, imprinted in our life chart, and we feel them in our solar plexus.

Remember, angels and spirit guides are truly the beloved messengers of God, and they are never to be replaced—not even by our loved ones who have passed over. And the true infusion of knowledge comes from God, so we can never, ever forget that Divine source.

CHAPTER 5

WHAT ABOUT DREAMS?

My clients have reported to me more times than I can count that they keep dreaming about this same entity who appears to them over and over to talk to them or deliver a message, and they want to know if it's an angel, a soul mate, or a disguised loved one. Well, it's none of the above. Not that we can't dream and get a valid message from angels and loved ones, but the so-called stranger who keeps showing up and leading you through situations is your spirit guide.

I have a client who, when he feels distressed, will dream of sitting on a park bench, and a tall, very artistic-looking male will come and sit with him and give him advice. Yet our guides' help is not always as direct as you might think, which can be strange. For example, as I mentioned earlier, the message I got from Francine before my first marriage was, "Are you sure you're doing the right thing?" This was more a thought-provoking question than a directive telling me what to do, and it was also very profound, psychologically. I don't mean to say that guides can't get adamant, especially in times of extreme stress or danger, but most often they'll communicate with you in a way that makes you rethink what you thought you were sure of.

A more clarified directive came to one of my clients one night when she dreamed she was at a party. She was surrounded by many people she knew when, all of a sudden, a young man in a long robe approached her. She thought how out of place he seemed to be: Everyone was in evening wear, and here was this man in a plain muslin robe. Anyway, he grabbed her arm, looked deep into her eyes, and said, "Don't let your son go to school tomorrow."

My client awakened and immediately checked on her seven-year-old, who was his usual happy self. He wasn't running a temperature, and nothing seemed amiss, but the dream really nagged at her. Finally, she gave in and reluctantly kept her son home, the whole time feeling that she probably needed to check herself in somewhere for an examination.

At about 10 A.M., the phone rang—another mother called her hysterically to report that the school bus her child would have been on had had a terrible accident, some children had died, and the rest were injured. Thank God my client listened to the message in her dream!

SEPTEMBER 11, 2001

There are so many stories that came out of the September 11, 2001, World Trade Center tragedy that it would take another book to report them all, but several people I've spoken with had dreams that told them to delay going to work—or not go at all—that day. In a strange way, some were even *blocked* from going to the city. Why were they spared when the rest were not? It's very simple: It wasn't their time, and their guides were making sure that they didn't leave before they were supposed to.

CHAPTER 6

YOUR QUESTIONS
ARE ANSWERED!

The following questions about spirit guides have been posed to me by readers of my books, by my clients, and by miscellaneous individuals over the years.

Q. Sylvia, how many spirit guides can a person have?

A. I've never found anyone in all of my years of research to have more than two guides. Even if that's the case, there's always a primary guide (such as Francine) who helps us with our written chart that we completed before we came into this life.

Q. Can guides ever move objects?

A. Guides have been known to move things, but this is rare. Since they're of such a high vibration, they can operate electrical items, such as making lights go on and off. I remember one client who did an exercise to get in touch with her guide, and soon afterward there was a loud popping noise that came out of the speakers of her television—and her TV was off!

Q. Do *we* ever become guides?

A. Yes, everyone gets the chance to be a guide. It isn't that complicated, except for studying the chart with the entity. We choose to help each other before we ever come into life.

Q. Why do some people have male guides while others have female guides?

A. Well, Francine says that it's related to our left and right brain. In other words, I have a female guide because I needed to expand my emotional side more. A male guide will be there if you need to balance your intellect. This doesn't mean that we're necessarily ineffectual in this area; it just gives us an extra boost.

Q. Can guides change our charts?

A. No, but they can help *modify* our chart, give solace during the pain, and often petition the Council to, let's say, give us some light at the end of the tunnel. Think of our guides as trusted friends who unconditionally love us and go through everything with us, who encourage us, and who aren't beyond giving us a gentle but effective kick in the backside.

Q. Can guides heal?

A. Our guides can heal and help us mentally, but they always call on angels or even "spirit doctors" to assist us. Because they're so advanced, the guides have the ability to call on any and all entities at their disposal.

Q. Do guides ever leave us?

A. No, our spirit guides never, ever leave us—they're with us every waking moment. They do have the ability to bilocate, though, which means that they're able to be in two places at the same time, in full consciousness. This is hard for our finite minds to comprehend, but on the Other Side, our essence is so strong that we can fully be in two places at once. For instance, a guide could be watching over you and still be before the Council pleading your case to modify your chart or get some advice or extra help.

Q. Can a guide be mistaken for a ghost or loved one who's passed over?

A. Rarely can a guide be mistaken for one of these entities, because he or she won't manifest in the same way. The reason we see ghosts is because they haven't made the transition to the Other Side and are therefore closer to this dimension. In the case of deceased loved ones, it takes a period of time after they pass to reach the elevated vibration level of guides, because they've so recently come from this dimension. If the guide does manifest, it will be a brief appearance, like when I actually saw Francine and Raheim. Instead, there's a real sense that they're with me, but not in full-body form.

Q. Do people share guides?

A. No, although guides can visit each other or get information from other guides. Many people have even tuned in to Francine briefly at my lectures. When I'm speaking, I always have this strong sense that many spirit guides are getting together and saying things such as, "If you think *you've* got problems, look at what I'm dealing with."

CHAPTER 7

SHARED EXPERIENCES WITH SPIRIT GUIDES

I've received countless stories from people who've written or e-mailed me via our website (www.sylvia. org) about their experiences with spirit guides. What follows are just a few of the most memorable ones.

Karen writes:

I was lying on my bed one night, and I was in complete despair. My husband, whom I'd loved and trusted for 15 years, had found another woman and was filing for divorce. I was so despondent that I wanted to die. I couldn't even imagine life without him. Just at my darkest moment, my eyes traveled to a small pinpoint of light. I wondered how there could be any light in a totally dark room, but as I watched, the light grew bigger and bigger. In the middle of the light stood this tall, beautiful man with dark, wavy hair and chiseled features. He smiled at me, and I heard him say, "Take heart. God has great things in store for you in six months."

I was still sad, but elated at the same time, and just as I was ready to respond, the vision disappeared. I told a few people, and they didn't believe me, but I know you will, Sylvia. [No kidding.] In exactly six months, I met a wonderful man who truly loves me, and I've been happily married now for four years.

Karen, this was definitely a guide who came to you during a time of great need. It's not often that someone will get a message foretelling future events, but due to your desperation, the guide probably got "clearance" to at least get a message of truth and hope to you.

Jason writes:

I was in my last year of college and couldn't figure out what I wanted to be. I had agonized about it for more than three years. I felt defeated and confused to the point that the depression was becoming overwhelming. My family seemed to be very irritated with me and was constantly asking me what I was going to be when I grew up.

I'd been obsessing over a term paper and could not seem to finish it. I just felt all dried up. I decided to take a nap, and I was in that half-asleep, half-awake state, when a beautiful blonde woman appeared before me and pointed at my unfinished term paper. I couldn't understand what she meant. Later, when I came to full consciousness, I saw that at the end of the half-finished paper was the word "doctor." It was in my handwriting, but I can't ever remember writing it. I am now a successful neurologist, but often wonder if it ever would have happened without that visitation.

Well, Jason, it *would* have happened. Your subconscious probably took over and wrote that word down, and the guide appeared to reaffirm that whether you knew it on a conscious level or not, your soul mind knew your chart, and your guide wanted to show up to validate what you charted yourself to do.

Brian writes:

When I was 45 years old, I had an unexpected heart attack. I was in intensive care and felt myself slipping away. As I did, I popped out of my body and looked down at myself being worked on by a team of doctors. I didn't seem to be that concerned; I was more curious. Then I became aware of a male presence that seemed to be in a white robe. He had long hair, was clean-shaven, and had the most compassionate eyes. For a split second I thought that this was Jesus, but then the figure approached me, and I got the distinct impression that the entity's name was Daniel.

I asked, "Who are you?" He said, "I have always been here to protect you, but you must go back. It is not your time." With that, I was back in my body.

Brian, many people believe that they see Jesus, and it isn't that they don't or can't, because I have many letters that attest to this. Jesus, like our guides, is always available to us, just as God is, but because you got the name "Daniel" and the explanation from this figure, it's clear that you were contacted by a guide. Guides will often show up in times of stress, and always come to take us Home to the Other Side during our final exit. It wasn't your time to leave this plane yet, Brian, and the guide made sure you didn't give up.

Janice writes:

One night I was fast asleep when I was awakened by a voice at about 3 A.M. It called my name and said, "Go to Joey." That's my nine-month-old son's name. I jumped out of bed and ran to his room, and there was Joey, pressed into the side of the crib—and he wasn't breathing. I was frantic, but I gave him mouth-to-mouth resuscitation until he began to cry. Now, Sylvia, the strangest part of this is that yes, I was highly emotional and full of fear, but even after going through that unbelievable, almost fatal incident, I had the feeling that everything would be all right.

Janice, two things were operating here. The guide called on you to help save Joey, and the energy and peace that the presence infused into you helped you get through that trauma.

Now, you may ask, "What about the chart?" Well, it was in her chart that Janice was supposed to go through this. While it would have been in Joey's chart, too, it was more for Janice's experience so that she could be aware that she was being helped and protected. Janice might have needed this affirmation to prove to her that someone was truly watching out for her and her son.

Some messages are more subtle. For example, there's a minister in my group who was going through a spiritual crisis, which is something that many of us experience, especially when we embark on the quest for truth. Although this woman wanted to be a minister, she felt that she wasn't good enough for it, and she felt overwhelmed and unworthy. Rather than face me, she decided to e-mail her resignation. She tried three times, but it wouldn't go through. To test her e-mail service, she sent several other people messages about different subjects with no problem. However, when it came to resigning, she couldn't make a connection. *I* know why (and now *she* knows, too) she was stopped from doing something drastic, and we both thank her guide for this.

Christen writes:

My mother died (I'd lost my father six months prior to that), and then my fiancé broke up with me. My job was also in jeopardy. I went home after a long day at work and decided that I was going to take a whole bottle of pills that I'd kept after my mother's illness. I got myself all ready, got into bed, put a glass of water by my bedside, put the pills in my hand, and started to put them in my mouth. All of a sudden, there was a strong breeze, and it was as if someone flipped my hand, sending pills all over the room. I sat transfixed, and out of the silence came a sweet, soft voice that said, "Don't. God is watching." I decided right then that there had to be another way to deal with my life. Shortly afterward, my life began to turn around.

Christen, your spirit guide was going to use whatever methods of communication she could to get her message across . . . and thank God she did.

And now, I'd like you to get to know *my* spirit guides in further detail. Part II will give you more information about Francine and Raheim, as well as how they spend their "time."

PART II

A DAY IN THE LIFE OF A SPIRIT GUIDE

CHAPTER 8

THEY KNOW US BETTER THAN WE KNOW OURSELVES

In one of my newsletters, I briefly referred to Francine's duties on the Other Side—it was just a more-or-less casual mention of what her life was like. Well, the result was a barrage of e-mails, letters, and phone calls from people asking me to tell them more about my spirit guide and theirs.

I began to realize that even though I've heard her for 61 years of my life, I didn't really know how Francine spent her time. Sure, I knew that she researches, goes to lectures, and checks in with the Hall of Records and Akashic Records, but that's about all the information I had.

While I was at a board meeting for Novus Spiritus recently, one of my cardinals said out of the blue that he'd run across a trance transcript in the archives that tells about the guides' duties. I hadn't said a word about the added section for this book—and besides, we were in the middle of talking about our new church branch that's starting in Canada. (It's funny, though, that the more the ministers are around me, the more they seem to pick up details from my life in a real, psychic way. It doesn't happen all the time, but often enough for me to realize what I've always said: The more spiritual you become, the more you're able to discern.)

When I began to write my books and open my church and foundation, I'm not going to lie to you—it took a lot of courage. I asked Francine, "What do I do about these vicious skeptics?" She said to just leave them alone because in some life they're going to find their knowledge or God-center. So over the years I've preferred not to deal with them, and after all, everyone has their own path to follow. I might have been a skeptic myself in some life, but I doubt it. I think we just know when God is firmly rooted in our soul; plus, as Francine says, there's so much phenomena left to be revealed before this planet's time is over that it's going to leave the naysayers in the dust.

She and I have conversations about God and religion and philosophy (it's a shame she never gave me answers for tests in college). When I heard about some miracles happening during the filming and show-ing of Mel Gibson's motion picture *The Passion of the Christ*, I asked, "Why now?" And she said, "Sylvia, miracles happen every day, for everyone, and it has been so since the beginning of Earth's time . . . people just happen to be recognizing them now, which also shows God's intervention. It's just now coming to the consciousness of humankind."

She's also told me that every guide feels a human-ized frustration when we go through a challenging time. For example, when I lost nine people in three months, Francine told the ministers that yes, I *had* charted this life, but the pain needed to ease up. Right on the heels of this, my third husband (who was also my friend of 32 years) asked for a divorce. We'd grown apart, and he'd also met someone else on a trip we'd taken to Turkey and Greece. Francine kept warning me all along that he might have seemed to be for me, but the marriage was really for *him*. Many people can't stand it when their partners are successful, especially if they come with grown children or grandchildren. They begin to feel that they're low on the totem pole.

Anyway, I hit the proverbial wall. Even though Francine had given me many subtle warnings, I was still so upset. I screamed, "Why didn't you tell me about this?!"

"Would you have believed me?" she asked.

"No . . . never about him," I admitted, and that's the oldest story in the universe, isn't it? It doesn't matter if you're psychic or not—your guide can't keep you totally protected from past-life ills or the lessons of this life. Yet he or she is always loving and patient with you, no matter what, and realizes that you have it hard down here. Your guide can and will ease the pain, as do God and your angels if you give it up to them.

Raheim told the ministers that Francine was at the Council continually petitioning for help with my feelings of rejection. (And she wasn't alone—guides line up daily to ask for more angels or more healing, along with intervention from Mother God, the Holy Spirit, Christ, and anyone they can think of to help their charges.) Meanwhile, she kept telling me that it wasn't worth all this pain because too many people needed and loved me, and grief is selfish. Of course that's true, but it doesn't mean that I didn't go through that pain.

I've gone on to ask her why those who do good are persecuted more than the bad entities of the world, and her answer was so reasonable: Who would care if a mean person was hurt (they never seem to be anyway)? This is their abode here, and we've all known them as mothers, fathers, friends, sisters, brothers, children, and, of course, husbands and wives. What better way to hurt you than to come close like Judas and then let the ax fall for 30 pieces of silver? But she said that if someone hurts another without warning or without giving them a chance to fix it, karma does engage, and it will come back to that person in five years or less. This is a great lesson for all of us.

Francine has told me many times that all the guides remark that the people they guide seem to remember the pain in life longer and more intensely than the joy. The reason is that this is a negative plane, and it is the home front of evil and deception. If it wasn't, we wouldn't learn.

Our guides always have our best interests at heart. In fact, every guide has been to visit every galaxy and gain information on how they handle such and such in their world that could relate to a problem we're facing. This gives spirit guides a fresh view of a problem and some advice on how to handle it. Francine has told me that very little is generated from these trips except experience because, as she told me when I was a young girl, this planet is the insane asylum of the universe—and the longer I live here, the more I just know that's true.

Even though our guides are very helpful and wise, we can argue with and even get mad at them . . . Lord knows I have. I've gone so far as to say, "So what in the hell are you doing to help me? Have you been on vacation or what?" And once when I was coming back from doing the *Montel* show, I was thinking about how hard traveling was getting for me, so I asked her (knowing full well the answer and also getting ready to be mad about it), "How was your day, Francine?"

Well, it so happened that she'd listened to a new composition by Mozart and heard a lecture on the war in the Middle East by Abraham Lincoln. Now I know how far-fetched this seems, but most of history's remarkable figures are on the Other Side, and everyone over there takes advantage of the great minds (as I certainly would).

Sometimes it's frustrating to hear about all the wondrous things and people at their disposal, while we're just poking along down here trying to learn in the best way we can. But Francine always says, as all guides try to convey to their charges, that everything will be over soon and I'll be Home, safe and sound. I'll look back at this as not only a learning place, but a bad memory.

IT'S A TEAM EFFORT

You may wonder why we even need a guide if we're just going to experience the rejection, grief, and abandonment of life anyway. Well, as Francine says (and I've really come to believe it), how much worse could it have been if they weren't there? Sure, you take the blows, but your guides take them with you and soften them more than you could imagine. The reason I know this is because the people who are aware of their guides seem to bounce back faster, get well quicker, and embrace life with more zest in a shorter amount of time.

I find that the wonderful thing about guides is that they don't all have to give us voice contact, as Francine does with me. (I've said many times that all people have psychic ability, but not all people are psychics.) Instead, they'll communicate with us through that "small voice inside" that warns us or tells us to go ahead. People get mad that they don't hear their little voice more . . . well, you do, trust me. It's just that our world has become so noisy and so full of stress that we don't listen to or hear it, and if we do it's too late.

Even though Francine doesn't give me too much personal information, there have been times when she's warned me or my family about something or even relayed messages to me about my staff or ministers. For example, she once told me to tell my dad to get his kidneys checked. Daddy, God love him, said, "I'm fine." A week later he was in the hospital with a kidney infection.

I also remember clearly when I met Ski at age 20, who was to become the love of my life. He was going to flight school in Kansas City, and I first saw him at a party at my house. He was tall, with black hair and green eyes, and his first words to me were, "You must be the hostess with the mostest," and he said my eyes were as big as silver dollars. In the late '50s, that was a winning line . . . I was a goner.

I'd gone upstairs to fix my hair, and as I stood there, Francine said, "This will be a hard tragedy in your life." I thought she meant my leaving a boyfriend I'd been going with—that it would hurt him. Like my clients, I didn't ask what she meant or how it would happen. Oh, the endorphins of love! Well, it came out after six months that Ski was married with two kids, and being a good Catholic girl, I sent him packing. I won't go into the pain, as we've all had it, but it's something I was meant to go through.

So guides do warn us. . . . I hate to admit this, but Francine had also worried about the cruelty of my first husband, yet she told me that the benefits of marrying him outweighed the bad, and they did. I had two wonderful boys and ended up moving to California. Kansas City was great, but I'm sure that I wouldn't have become so well known in Missouri. So no matter how bad it seems, your chart will enact itself.

Keep in mind that we have five exit points, times when we can get out of life through an accident, a near-death experience, and so forth. I can't tell you how many times I've seen or been told that our guides deflect these, but most of them wait for the last exit point.

I had my first exit point at age 26. I almost died from hepatitis A, but Francine told me that I wasn't ready to go. Another one was when I had an operation for removal of my uterus many years later—in fact, I was actually going through the tunnel toward the light and was called back by one of the nurses who was a dear friend (at least she was until she called me back . . . just kidding) and knew of my philosophy. Guess what words she used to do the dastardly deed? Yep, "People need you!" I think it's becoming my theme song. (A few years later, I was having another surgery, and my heart stopped.)

And then the strangest thing happened last summer. I was riding in my youngest son's boat when a huge ski board came loose and whirled around and hit me in the head. I didn't think much about it except for the fact that it hurt like hell and gave me a big knot and bruise. Later Francine said that she directed the angels around me to deflect it, because a few more inches over and it would have hit my temple, and guess what . . . lights out permanently, because I only have one more exit point left.

Every guide (who I know for sure is the dearest, most loyal friend you'll ever have), says that they'd never be a guide again—yet they know us better than we know ourselves. For example, when I told Francine years ago that I'd never charge for missing people or emergency crises, she said, "I know."

Like a dummy, I asked, "*How* do you know?"

"Because," she replied, "I know you."

Over the years, this has been an on-again, off-again refrain. Our guides know us: our likes and dislikes and if we're getting in too deep, and the more we rely on them or even believe that they exist, it makes them get to us easier and help us more. They can't change our chart, and if we go too far off track they just wait patiently for us to cross over, where they'll then take us to the Hall of Wisdom and show us where we missed the signposts.

When we get Home, our guides comfort us while we scan our life and rejoice over our accomplishments—there isn't any criticism except from us. Then we go over our chart and note what we would have done differently or even how well we did in this life we just lived, and this is when we decide to come back or not. Francine says that most of us won't come back but will go on to be spirit guides ourselves.

Of course, this book wouldn't be complete without talking about Raheim, the guide I acquired (or I should say "began to know about") around 1970. Francine says that many guides have a mentor, and Raheim is hers. Now everyone's going to start asking me who their guide's mentor is! Well, I don't know. I know the guides, but I'm certainly not privy to every-one they meet with or talk to. I do know that guides discuss things with the Council and other guides and that they confer with God and the angels, but they also usually have a master teacher who has a cer-tain expertise that's in accordance with the person they're guiding.

For instance, a healer may have a doctor on the Other Side who helps them, or a sculptor will get an advanced artist to infuse them, or what have you. Not only do these master teachers enhance the abilities that entities come down into life with, but they also help fortify them. I don't think anyone, including me, realizes what an intricate team effort this is.

Now I'd like to give you the details of how I "met" both Francine and Raheim.

©Christina Simonds

CHAPTER 9

MEETING FRANCINE
AND RAHEIM

There are some things that stand out in your mind with such sharpness that it's as if it happened yesterday. . . .

I was seven years old, and it was a beautiful spring day in Kansas City. My mother and father were at work; my sister, Sharon, was with her friend Dorothy; and my beloved Grandma Ada was outside.

I was upstairs in our Queen Anne home, standing in my room brushing my bushy, unruly hair. (Actually, I was just trying to act busy so I wouldn't have to go downstairs and help Grandma in her victory garden.) I don't know how to explain it, but it was as if someone had stepped behind me. The presence was so real that I kept staring in the mirror, expecting to see someone.

Now you have to realize that from the time I was three years old, I could foresee the future, such as the death of my grandfather, and I knew who was coming over before they even rang the doorbell. At age five I saw both of my great-grandmothers' faces run like melting wax, and in two weeks both were dead. As a child, seeing faces run—and then having these people die shortly thereafter—was very frightening and traumatic, but it finally ended when my grandmother told me to ask God to take it away.

At night I had to have a light on or use the flashlight that Grandma Ada gave me because I'd see people from the Other Side coming and going in my room. So what I'm saying is that this second sight wasn't necessarily a new thing. Since I always had it, it seemed natural to me . . . but I'd never had any voice contact before. I guess as I look back, vision was all right or at least bearable, but a voice was another sensory phenomenon that I had yet to deal with.

Anyway, as I looked in the mirror with this overwhelming sense of a presence, one of the most defining moments of my life happened: A high-pitched voice with fast, clipped words said, "I come from God, I am here to guide and protect you, and you don't have to be afraid." For a brief instant, every hair on my body seemed to stand on end. At first I felt rooted to the spot, but then I dropped the brush and went screaming down the stairs, two steps at a time, and out the back door.

My grandmother stared up at me, and I must have looked a fright—I was near the point of hysteria. Dear Grandma, with her soft arms and ever-present lavender smell, grabbed me and held me tight. "Sylvia," she said, "what is it?"

"A voice!" I managed to hoarsely croak out (yes, I've always had a hoarse voice). "I heard a voice!"

"So," she gently asked, "what did it say?" I told her, and she held my face in both of her rough but well-manicured hands and said, "Honey, we've talked about this many times . . . this is your Control [the old Spiritualist word for *guide*]. Wasn't it a female?"

"I think so."

"Well, we come from a long line of hearing voices, and now you have yours. You're very fortunate to hear her," my grandmother calmly said. Then she added, "She's Indian, I think."

"How do you know?" I asked (I sounded like my clients).

"Because I'm psychic, too," she said patiently, "and I've caught sight of her a time or two."

"Why didn't you tell me?"

"It's better to let you come into your own," she said matter-of-factly. "Ask her what her name is."

"I don't want her!" I retorted. "I want to be alone without someone hanging around."

"We all have them," she said. "You just happened to hear yours."

"I won't talk to her!" I spat, stamping my foot.

Grandma Ada smiled that knowing smile I loved, but that at times like this made me want to scream. "Then get the shovel and dig up those carrots and radishes," she said, as if the conversation was over.

Later on in the evening as I was going to bed, Grandma sat down next to me. She said, "Sylvia, we come from a very long line of people who have this ability: my mother, my brother, my mother's mother, and so on before her."

"So how does that make me feel better?"

"Because God gave it to you, and you have to use it for good," she replied.

"I'm not going to use any of it," I stubbornly said, "and no one can make me!"

"We'll see," she answered, giving me that "I've got a secret" smile.

Little by little over the next few months, Francine would say a few things to me. In those days she was almost motherly, saying things like, "You don't want to say that, do you?" or "There isn't any reason to be cross." She wasn't scolding and not really admonishing, and she just shared a few sentences at first.

As I look back, I realize how clever Francine was, because she'd play a game with me that I'll call "spy."

I'd be upstairs, and my two grandmothers and Rosie, our maid, would be downstairs, let's say; or Mom and Dad would come home from work and be talking in the kitchen; or even if my sister was on the phone—Francine would start telling me the conversations they were having, and then at dinner I'd flabbergast everyone by repeating what they'd said.

Sometimes today I wish that Francine would play "spy" again, but she never does. She stated that it was all right back then because she was establishing validity, but there's a privacy act that God governs. Even looking back, the stuff she told me was so banal, such as Sharon's homework, Dad griping about work, Mom just griping. . . . It was never anything that I wouldn't or couldn't have heard, but it all had enough detail to make us take notice.

Gradually, having a spirit guide just seemed to fit into my life. I've always been aware of Francine, but she's never made me feel self-conscious. In fact, there are private moments in our lives that are domed, meaning that our guides can't see or hear what we do, but they're always there. Like our angels, they never leave us.

I began to sit in with Grandma Ada, and the more I did, the more I learned. People lined up to see her:

ministers, priests, women with babies, men who had gotten off of work, and so forth. Sometimes she'd lay her hands on them, while other times she'd just speak to them.

We'd talk about it later, and she'd ask me to tell her my impressions. She always said to remember that "what goes on in here or wherever you are stays between you and God and the people you help." Not only was this about psychic etiquette, it was a real moral lesson, too. I also learned that even though Francine had a voice, she'd never help me with my readings. My grandmother had several voices, and they didn't help her either. They gave out philosophy, and once in a great while a jewel of information was dropped, but as far as verbal guidance goes—no. However, I know that guidance comes in a form of nudging along the way.

RAHEIM

If I want to know something and Francine doesn't know, she'll tell me that she's going to confer with Raheim or the Council. But 9 times out of 10 she goes to Raheim.

Raheim looks very much like Korla Pandit (the organist who was on TV in the '50s, for those of you who remember). Now here's what's interesting: Even though I haven't wanted to see Francine (although I have at brief intervals), I saw Raheim in living color when my boys and I were living in a tenement to get away from my husband, who threatened to kill us. I was putting my boys to sleep, and Mary, my adopted daughter, was in the kitchen. I happened to look in the front room, and there he was: beautiful, tall, bronze, with a pointed snow-white turban and Nehru jacket. He almost seemed embarrassed that I'd seen him . . . and then he was gone.

Although I've seen Raheim, I've never had voice contact with him. You see, I only know of him through Francine, who told me that he's very philosophical and wise and is highly intelligent. He was a Sikh who lived in the year 800 C.E., and he was a teacher. Even though he was born in India and was an instructor of Hinduism, he felt that it didn't answer his needs, so he became a student of Gnosticism, which he calls the "old religion."

Once I was doing a reading for a very advanced spiritual Indian who I knew was a Sikh, and out of curiosity I asked, "Have you ever heard of a master teacher who lived around the year 800 by the name of Raheim?"

His mouth dropped open, and I swear if he were Christian he might have made the sign of the cross. "Of course, madam," he said very respectfully. "He is known to us as a great and holy teacher." (Well . . . who knew?)

Like Francine, Raheim comes in when I trance, and he's an expert in so many things: He's helped us with medicine, predictions, history, religion, and natural magic (which is his forte), among other subjects. In no way will I ever say that he's smarter than Francine—he just approaches everything from a more linear position because he's male. In the beginning, I think it was very hard for him to come into a woman's body. I'm told that when he came in the first time, he spent several moments examining my long fingernails and then remarked, "How can she do anything with these?"

One time I forgot and wore a skirt, and he was not too happy with that bit of feminine clothing because he crosses his legs and puts his hands together and bows his head. This is the Hindu form of a polite and spiritual greeting that signifies the recognition of the soul within each person.

I'm sure that he isn't too keen on coming into my body at all, but he does it for research purposes. And what's interesting is that even though he's in my human female body during trance, there are so many women who have said time and again that all that fades and they seem to see, sense, or feel the strength and intellect of this wonderful, advanced male entity.

Raheim sits up and moves my body more than Francine, I'm told. (I can't stand to see a video of myself in trance. How would you like to watch what looks like you . . . but isn't?!) But he isn't very good at answering personal questions because he's simply not as humanized as Francine. For example, if you were to ask Francine about a pet dog that had passed over, she'd answer that it had made the transition, was fine, and was waiting to greet you on the Other Side when *you* passed over. Raheim, on the other hand, would probably just say that it died. He's not trying to be cruel; he's simply very matter-of-fact—it's merely a different way of male and female delivery. So he really doesn't do personal trances, but his information is magnificent.

According to Francine, Raheim's expertise is alchemy, and he's done tremendous research on physical and mental health and intuitive magic. Now this isn't the type of magic that you think: no spells, cauldrons, and so on. It really boils down to what the ancient shamans believed: If you want rain, pour water into the earth. In other words, if you believe hard enough, miracles can happen. Life imitates thoughts, and we become what we believe magically.

Raheim is very much into the tools of protection, and Francine says that he can do more physical phenomena than she can. I experienced this firsthand when I was in the mountains of Silver Lake, California, with my second husband, Dal. We were staying at the Kit Carson Lodge, in a cabin that was separate from the main building. As we were inclined to do in those days, Dal and I were discussing parapsychology, and the conversation got around to physical phenomena. On somewhat of a lark, we both challenged Francine and Raheim to make something physical happen. We did this even though we were pretty sure that nothing *would* happen—after all, we'd asked them before, to no avail. In fact, we had a little private joke that we always used to utter about moving objects, which was simply, "The object is moving so fast that it looks like it's standing still!" Needless to say, Francine and Raheim didn't necessarily appreciate our humor.

Now, neither Francine nor Raheim are physical guides like those of physical mediums. You see, while I'm a spiritual medium, some physical mediums can actually move objects and create physical phenomena with the help of their guides. Well, I'm here to tell you that both my guides put on a show that night that would have put anything or anyone on this planet to shame.

As Dal and I settled on the bed to watch "the challenge," it was totally dark outside, and I mean *dark*: There were no outside lights, there was no moon out, and we were in a secluded place in the mountains. Francine told me to turn off the lights in the cabin, so Dal and I were in total blackness, cracking jokes and giggling like kids.

All of a sudden, a white ball of light appeared on the wall opposite our bed . . . and the giggling stopped. The ball started to elongate up the wall in a line about six inches wide, and both of us were flabbergasted as we watched this light grow in intensity and brightness. Being scientific researchers and always skeptical in an open-minded sense, we thought that there must be some light coming in through the drawn curtains. Dal checked all the windows and doors and even went outside to find the source of this light—there was none.

The light was now very bright to our sight and making its way up the wall and across the ceiling in a straight line, but amazingly, it didn't illuminate the room that much. We were still in semidarkness, even though that light was getting steadily brighter. I was also getting excited chatter from Francine about what Raheim was doing to make the light grow in intensity and size. She told me to have Dal walk through a certain portion of the room. When he did, he said, "Oh my God! I just walked through someone!" He did it again and got the same feeling. That's because Raheim was standing there.

Dal was amazed and almost delirious because of the light and the feeling of a spirit body. Then, as Francine was smugly chattering away in my ear about Raheim's prowess, she told me to have Dal try to give energy while standing in the middle of Raheim's body. He did so, and the light immediately got even brighter and started to pulsate.

Forty-five minutes later, the light was now coming from the floor of the opposite wall, and it went up the wall and fully across the ceiling—and it was so bright and throbbing. I had a totally excited and fascinated husband, who was acting like an ecstatic kid checking for light sources again; an "I told you so" guide busily talking in her high-pitched frenzy about how Raheim seemed to be getting brighter and brighter and how she was getting concerned about him; and I was getting, in a word . . . *bored*. I'd had enough—after all, how long can you watch a stream of light in your room without manifesting some impatience with it all?

I said, "Okay, that's enough for now." I got an immediate "What?!" and a pout from my husband and an ever-increasing shrill, concerned voice in my ear, something about Raheim perhaps blowing up.

I smiled at Dal and said, "Raheim is expending too much energy, so we have to stop." He reluctantly said okay, and I told Francine to have Raheim stop. By this time she was really agitated and said, "I don't know if he can!" She then said that Raheim was going out to the lake to try to release the pent-up energy. The light immediately went out, and we were in total darkness again. Francine said, "I'll be right back," and finally her incessant chatter ceased. I had a headache that would make God want an aspirin.

A short time later Francine told me, "Everything is okay. Raheim was able to dissipate the energy over the lake, although some man in a boat got very frightened by seeing all these balls of light suddenly appearing and disappearing in the water." She went on to say that she'd been concerned because Raheim had gotten "overloaded" with energy and was almost like a whirling dervish out on the water. I relayed what she said to Dal, and we both laughed—but we were also very concerned.

Francine says that Raheim is often on call and has always given her the answers she wanted or needed. They both stick to my chart (as all our guides do), but one is more emotional and humanized, while the other is more linear. One time Raheim told a group that Francine was very upset about a critical point in my life and that she had to go to the Council to be comforted. The Council explained to her that I'd chosen this situation, but Francine petitioned that I'd had enough and had learned and fulfilled it (the test), so she asked that they make it stop. Raheim explained after this that it did begin to ease off a bit, which proves that yes, we learn our lessons, but the guides can go to the Council and scream "Uncle!"

I also know that they have what they call special "feast days" that celebrate events. One is Christ coming Home after being on Earth. No wonder . . . and how happy he must have been to come Home after the way he was treated. He had four guides and throngs of angels, but you see, even *he* had to go through suffering—all to bring about the aspect of a loving God.

CHAPTER 10

THE TRANCE EXPERIENCE

At this point I'd like to take a moment to explain about the trance state. If I'm in it, Francine is a virtual fountain of information about past lives, the Other Side, God, the life of Christ, mysteries, creation, and even personal questions. For example, one of my ministers once asked her if I'd have any more surgeries or serious illnesses (aside from when I die, of course). She said yes, that when I get older my right hip will bother me because my first husband threw me into a door.

So now my hip does give me problems every so often. I told her awhile back, "I thought you said when I get older."

She replied, "And how old are you?" Damn . . . I'm 68, but I didn't realize that I'm officially "older"!

Aside from this specific instance, Francine tends to be concise but vague when it comes to me. I know why she doesn't give me more direction, although it took me years to figure it out. If I depended on her, I wouldn't learn, and I wouldn't have developed my own ability—instead, I would have relied on her to tell me *everything*.

To this day, I get people on the phone asking if they're talking to me or Francine, and I always have to reply that it's just me. But never mistake the fact that I know I'm only a "tube" by which the information comes through from God. If it's wrong, it's because I'm not interpreting it right—I've always said that the human vehicle is flawed, and God is the only one who's right all the time. (Personally, and I've said this often, I think it would be scary to be right all the time.) I will say this, though: A psychic better be on the mark more often than not, and he or she better be right more often than wrong. As for me, I just hit hard and fast with the truth that I know rather than badgering people with a lot of questions. (Beware: This is done by many psychics, but it's really an unprofessional practice known as "fishing.")

I'm the only one I know of in my family who's had the ability to go into trance, except for Uncle Henry (who used to belong to the old Spiritualist camps in Florida). Grandma Ada didn't have the ability, nor does my psychic son, Chris. Trance mediumship is almost a forgotten ability in this day and age, and very few psychics have the ability to go into a deep trance state. Some say that they channel, but it's been my experience that this isn't really the true trance mediumship practiced by Edgar Cayce, Arthur Ford, and myself.

Of course, being a trance medium means that your guide (not maliciously) will tell stories about your life to make a point. For example, when Arthur Ford's guide, Fletcher, would come into his body, he'd tell everyone how much Arthur drank. It wouldn't be pleasant to have that blurted out. Thank God I haven't suffered with any kind of slippage from Francine . . . besides, I can't drink, and I have a hell of a time taking any pills or medications. She did say at one trance that I was drinking too much coffee, so I cut way back (I swear, everything you love is a no-no).

The first time I ever went into trance was when I was 19 years old. I was taking a class on hypnosis at the University of Kansas City, which was very progressive in the 1950s. I was sitting between two friends, and when I came to they were just staring at me. Everyone else in the class had left, but my friends were babbling about who I said I was and all that I'd told them. Now they'd both grown up with me, but they hadn't seen a trance, and more important, they hadn't seen *me* trance!

I, however, was livid because of the religious dogma that had been pounded into me—that is, the fear of being possessed and going to hell (remember, I had that Catholic background). Francine assured me that it would never happen again without my permission, but she had to show me that no harm came to anyone in trance, and it was sometimes easier to get her message across by using *my* vocal cords instead of her own high-pitched voice. To this day, she's kept her word.

Even though she did get my permission, I still had a hard time letting Francine come in and talk through me at first. However, I've never known her to hurt or coerce anyone or to use her skills for her own or my benefit. As she told me when I was very young, "If you ever misquote me for your own gain, it will be the end of all your abilities." I never thought of that, nor would I compromise my integrity. No matter what the prize was, it would never be worth it.

In many ways, I'm self-conscious about the trancing part of my ability, even after all these years. Why? Maybe because I've always approached life, as anyone who knows me can attest to, with either a scientific or practical sense, as well as the spiritual.

Once after I'd asked, "Why me?" Francine responded, "Sylvia, isn't your motive purely to help people and give them honest information as you get it?" I said, "Of course. You know that." So then she said, "Then why don't you get that in your head and go with it?"

That's when I began to somewhat relax (as much as you can with psychic ability) and make my own contract with God: that I'd never intentionally hurt anyone or keep anything back, and that I'd do it all with my ego out of the way. I've never had a problem with my ego—I don't take myself seriously, but I do take my gift very seriously. And whatever goes on with me personally never seems to affect my ability, thank God.

Now, you can certainly channel *without* going into trance. To tell you the truth, after an hour of Francine's high-pitched chirp, I'm ready to flee. But she can't help it—the sound quality, as I stated earlier, has to do with the warp in transmitting messages from their dimension to ours. And sometimes when she talks in my right ear, I have an affectation of moving my hand in a waving fashion, which means, *That's enough now, no more chatter*. However, if I've given you the impression that she's constantly talking, that would be erroneous, because she isn't. She only communicates when she has something important to say.

When Francine first started communicating through me in trance, she really had a problem with our slang. For example, a woman asked her why she'd been "stood up," and Francine answered that she didn't understand—what was wrong with standing up? Or someone mentioned a garage sale, and Francine wanted to know how you could just sell a garage. Even now she gets stumped at times, and that's why we always say when talking to guides that you don't have to talk in a special way, but the more literal you are the more they'll understand, because guides don't do well with double meanings or ambiguities.

Many times, spirit guides don't understand our humor either—in fact, Francine and Raheim both agree that humor is time-bound and is directly related to our media or our lives. And you know, as much as I loved my grandmother (and what a brain she had), she thought that a woman who used her false teeth to crimp the edge of a pie was hysterical. Granted, it is funny, but maybe it would have been funnier if, as we say so often, you'd been there. Anyway, if it hadn't been for my blessed, loving Grandma Ada (who was as close to a saint as I'll ever know in this life) and her patient, unconditional love . . . God knows how long it would have taken me to accept my ability.

I was the only one out of our long hereditary line of psychics to ever get tested. Grandma kept asking me, "Why don't you leave it alone?" Well, I'd decided to become a teacher, but I didn't want to do it if I was schizophrenic. As far as I was concerned, we could have all been a lineage of crazy people that no one figured out. So I was tested several times by three psychologists and one psychiatrist. They all came up with the same verdict: I was "normal," but had some type of paranormal ability that was unexplained.

I've also been tested numerous times while in trance. I've been poked and prodded, and had various scientific instruments hooked up to me and countless psychological tests given to me (or I should say, Francine), and still much can't be explained. An electro-encephalogram (EEG) was hooked up to me, and when Francine entered, all the lines on the monitoring sheet stopped (which means death), there was a blank place on the sheet, and then the pattern continued after she was fully in my body. EEG machines can monitor the pure alpha state (a meditative state of brain-wave activity) I enter into when Francine is using my body and talking.

To digress here a moment, I've also been tested with a machine that was hooked up to a toy dog that barked (God, I've done some crazy things in my life). The premise was that the dog would bark whenever anyone hooked up to it would go into an alpha state, or the deeper states of theta brain-wave activity, and the person hooked up would, because of the distraction of the barking dog, come out of that altered state to the conscious state of beta brain-wave activity. In other words, the toy dog was supposed to measure a meditative or trance state, and when the person who was hooked up attained this state, they'd be prevented from maintaining it because of the barking noise. Once the conscious state of beta brain waves was reached, the dog would stop barking.

This experiment was conducted on a local community TV broadcast by a skeptical scientist who wanted to prove that an altered state of consciousness could not be maintained with distraction. They hooked me up, I talked with my eyes open . . . and all the while the dog kept barking. The scientist was beside himself and kept saying, "This doesn't happen!" He went back to the drawing board, perplexed by how I could do this. He should have known that many monks and yogis can maintain altered states of consciousness with distraction and noise around them. Anyway, this was just a little humorous true story, but now back to my doing trances.

Pictures have been taken with special film when Francine was coming into my body and I was going out (we still have the photos in our research files). When she came in, there was a funnel of pure light going into the top of my head, while when I was going out it looked like sparkly flecks dispersed out of my head. Francine even named the frames of film in which this phenomenon occurred and would be visible. When I looked at the pictures, I asked her why I looked so scattered, and she told me that the soul does this, but then it condenses right away and gains strength.

It's still disconcerting to feel that you're all scattered, but that only happens for a moment in trance, not when we die. Earlier I used to wonder if I'd come back from the trances, and over the years it's given some people as well as my ministers some worry that I wouldn't. I have to tell you, in dark times it began to enter my mind that that wouldn't be such a bad idea, but sure enough, I've come back every time.

While the trance experience is certainly exciting and fun for those who witness it, it's neither for me. First of all, I feel like everyone is going to a party, but I have to go to bed. Also, the process is like falling into a deep well with no sound, much like losing consciousness. I'm told that I go to the Other Side and sit (gee, that sounds like fun), but I don't remember anything that happens while I'm in a trance state. When I come out, I'm dizzy and disoriented, but I've also gone into trance with an upset stomach, a crunching headache, and a fever of 102 degrees and come out feeling great . . . so there's a great benefit as well. It's as if Francine leaves a healing essence as a thank you for the use of my body.

When my dear friend Montel Williams witnessed me trance, he stated afterward that it was one of the most informative and spiritual experiences he'd ever had. He's never told me what was said to him and six other people (nor has Francine!). I really don't want to know—it's none of my business anyway.

People say that when I'm in trance for a while, my eyes change and darken, my face gets flatter, and my features change. I'm told that my voice doesn't change that much (and that's logical, since my guides are using my vocal cords), but the manner of speech and usage of the language changes considerably, and it most definitely sounds like someone else is talking through me.

CHAPTER 11

IN FRANCINE'S
OWN WORDS

Next you're going to hear from Francine herself. This is a little slow going for me because I can only stand so much of her talking to me. Now you may wonder, "After all these years, why does it bother you?" Well, even though she and I do talk, it tends to be in spurts. Usually I trance for this type of book, but I felt it was more personal if she and I did this chapter together, since we've been through so much over the years. So anything I felt like commenting on is in brackets . . . you know me, I'm always going to give my two cents' worth!

Francine: My real name is Iena, but Sylvia has chosen to call me Francine, which I don't mind. She has always tried to validate what I have said and who I am, but I understand. This is what has kept her practical and on track, even though she is so stubborn. *[No comment.]*

I am about 5'9" and slender. I have almond-shaped eyes and am olive skinned. I have jet-black hair, which I usually keep in a thick braid that almost comes to my waist. I tend to wear, as most female guides do, loose-fitting, flowing dresses; and my favorite colors are blue, gold, and green.

I have always had consciousness of my being alive. I lived in Colombia, South America, from 1500 to 1519. I was married when I was 13 and had a baby girl when I was 14½. My husband's name was Serri, and he was an Aztec priest. I was of cross blood: Aztec and Inca. *[I didn't believe she could be both, but I consulted several historians and they said that during that time and prior, there was a definite mixing of Aztecs and Incas.]*

When I was in life, my guide was a male named Larne who had been an Inca priest many centuries before my life. I could hear him at times in my mind and get strong feelings from him, but I truly didn't live long enough to get into hearing him audibly. The Aztecs and Incas believed that their ancestors were their guides—when I came back Home I realized that this wasn't true, but Larne was just as effective to have with me.

I was killed with a spear in my heart because I ran out in the road to save my daughter from marauding soldiers. She was eventually okay and raised by another family. From my dimension *[the Other Side]* I watched her grow up and marry and have children. My husband was also killed, but he joined me here soon after.

You may ask why I had only one life and was still advanced enough to receive my assignment with Sylvia. I don't always know what the Council and God have in store—I just know that we are picked because we have the strength, disposition, personality, and spirituality to fit with our charges. I was told by the Council that I would have to train for a long time to be a verbal and vocal spirit guide for an entity that came from a long lineage of psychics.

Now our time is not your time—three or four hundred of your years is like weeks over here—but the training was intense. *All* guide training is very intense, and some don't choose to do what is required to be a communicating guide, which I had to go through and is even more involved. During my training, I met a master teacher named Raheim who said that he would help me. He became my mentor (along with God and the Council).

Usually entities on their last lives end up on the sixth level *[the highest level of individuality on the Other Side]*, which is the level of orientators *[those who help people coming in and out of incarnations]*, teachers, lecturers, and spirit guides. The chances of all "last lifers" ending on the sixth level is about 90 percent, and most usually end up being guides.

Many people would like to believe that they have had lives with their guide, but this is more of a rarity than the rule. Spirit guides are never your family members, because they have to be training long before your lineage has started. Your loved ones who have passed over become like loving protectors, but the guide is the one in charge, so to speak.

Anyway, I had to augment my training by learning how to get into Sylvia's body without harming any organs and to learn to use her voice box. All of the guide training is geared toward the individual we will be guiding in life, so there are always small differences or nuances that we are trained in according to the person we will be guiding and what they want to accomplish in their chart.

All guides have to be humanized, and the process is quite painful. You see, we have just come back from hell (the Earth plane) and now we have to become more emotional and feeling—a process that angels are saved from. They stay in their heavenly bliss and just protect. We guides, on the other hand, have to have feelings; otherwise we wouldn't be of any use to the ones we are guiding. We must be able to sustain pain and loss, yet it is so much like Sylvia says: that the viewing of it is different from the actual human experience of living it. For example, when I had viewed my life before I came into Columbia, it seemed fine that I would live like a princess and die at 19. After I got in my life, even though I was of the upper class, it was very hard.

I would like to say in defense of my people that I never saw or heard of any sacrifices or hearts being ripped out, nor did we ever know of such things except in symbolism: It meant giving your heart to God. A small animal was laid on your chest on high holy days such as the Equinox, and the heart was then taken out of the animal to stand in for you and the giving of your blood. Nevertheless, we did go through attacks from other cultures. I lost my mother and father early, and experiencing grief as a human being is much different from viewing written words on your chart.

Please understand that even though we all know each other on the Other Side, we are not all close. I knew of Sylvia (who at that time was named Elizabeth) and had seen her at lectures and orientation, but I had never had a real conversation with her until we started meeting to discuss our roles in her next incarnation. She was about 5'6", had reddish hair, and was full figured. *[Damn!]* She had lived 53 lives up to this point, and this was to be her 54th. No one ever throws up the fact that so-and-so has had more lives than another—it's just the job of everyone to accelerate their spirituality for God. Sylvia was always surrounded by people and making them laugh, whereas I am more quiet and not as flamboyant. We do keep our same personalities over here, but we are in total joy and bliss at all times. We can also take on the looks of a life we loved. For a time Sylvia had Asian features because she enjoyed her looks in an Asian life. Did we all know who she was? Of course. We all have a small flaw in our appearance (such as the slight chip in my tooth or the small white "skunk lock" Sylvia has in front of her reddish hair), which is really more of a symbol of the fact that we are not perfect instead of a defect.

When we first met in the Hall of Justice, I felt that Sylvia really cared about me but thought I was too reserved. Gradually, though, we both realized that we were a good complement for one another. She was more the "live life on full tilt" type, while I was more conservative . . . it made a nice balance. Our phrases to each other were: "Oh, loosen up" (hers) and "Calm down" (mine).

We met often to plan, as do all entities in our situation. We also met with master teachers and the Elders of the Council, read other records, and planned and planned. The problem with Sylvia was that she picked an "example" option life, so her chart was different from most entities—not better or more advanced necessarily—in that she chose to come down for a specific mission. All entities have a mission in a sense, and everyone can take an option life, but these are the hardest to track. The only saving grace in Sylvia's convoluted chart was that she had been psychic in other lives.

As I have read in her past charts, she was not too thrilled about those either: She was isolated, burned, scorned, and so on. The Council promised that she would go through tests that were unbelievably hard, but she would not encounter any violence this time. *[Well, there are many ways to be crucified.]* The fact that she had a dark entity as her mother was a real bone of contention with me, but the Council convinced me that light comes through dark to overcome it. Every guide balks at having their charges come into darkness, but we are usually over-ruled because of the learning process.

We are the ones who petition Mother and Father God, the Council, and the angels when things get too rough for our charges. We don't always win, but we have been able to soften blows and even help with miracles and intervene moderately in the chart to help keep them on track. Even if people don't hear our voices, they get feelings, premonitions, hunches . . . sure, some of them come from God, but so many times we are the conduit by which messages come through.

Unfortunately, the hubbub of life keeps the mind too noisy. Most guides are overwhelmed right now, as so many of them have guided people when everyone lived more simply and were closer to nature, and they weren't so full of depression and anxiety. The world has gradually become so stressful within your time of 50 years. We all discuss what a frantic state everyone on Earth is in and how everyone tries so hard to keep up. It's the same thing that Sylvia used to say when she would see people rushing by her when she was driving: You still meet them at the stoplight. I always tell Sylvia to try to maintain a quiet center she can go to, even if it is just a room she creates in her mind. Of course, she doesn't always do it. . . .

I promised Sylvia now that I wouldn't get preachy *[yeah, right!]*, but all of us guides wish that in your world you would do things more slowly. We find that as life progresses, most of you go at a frenetic rate. We have wondered if you will eventually figure out what you are rushing toward. What is so paramount that you have to get it done with such immediacy? Watch people in stores race up and down the aisles, only to rush outside to load the car to go home, put everything away, and sit down. We find sometimes that it's very comical. We are not making fun of you, but sometimes it reminds one of an anthill.

You would probably say, "I have to do things like this so that they're over and done with," but do it more slowly. Give yourself time . . . there is another day, and if there isn't it won't matter to you anyway. You will still have enough time, and you won't be nearly as exhausted. You have a saying in your world that we like: "Stop and smell the flowers" [I think it's roses], but you don't. Now you won't want to come to the end of your life and feel that you didn't see the clouds or a beautiful sunset, smile at a baby, marvel at the red of the apple in the store, or smell an orange.

We guides live in the total serenity of single-mindedness, and that is the focus on our charges. We consult other guides when something arises that calls for it. If a situation is similar, we compare charts and ask for their advice. I guess for the sake of convenience, when our charges are asleep we take the mental notes we have made on them and consult with the Council. This can be anything from illness to problems going on in the ones we are guiding.

I know that it's hard to understand how we can go to the Council and still be with our charge. Yes, we can bilocate, but our dimension is right on top of yours, and our viewing and seeing ability, as well as listening acuity, is more than you can understand. It's true in human life that you only use 20 percent of your soul or physical mind, but here we use 100 percent, which affords us the ability to be in several places at once, have our senses attuned to you, and in essence, never leave your side.

If you even have too many bad dreams, we try to regulate them if asked. We call extra angels if you need them. If you have a bad cell memory, we try to push that to the front so that you'll have God release it. But please let me make this clear: We are just helpers to God—in no way do we ever take the place of Mother or Father God or our Lord.

As spirit guides, even though we train to become more humanized, we still live on the Other Side while we take care of you. There is no night on the Other Side, but some entities that are just back from life (or those who just like night) may create it for themselves. We are capable of creating many things on the Other Side, such as buildings, gardens, and so on, just by using our minds. Our temperature stays about 78 degrees, so it is very comfortable.

As far as our sexuality is concerned, any entity can merge with another if both choose to do so. It's hard to describe in finite language, but our essence can merge with another entity, and with this comes an euphoric, orgasmic feeling as well as absorbing their experiences from their lives. We gain wisdom this way and are also invited to watch someone's life if we want to really understand a certain aspect of it. We also hear lectures from people, as well as their guides, on how certain situations were handled so that we can also gain knowledge and learn.

Although our dimension is right on top of yours and for the most part is configured much the same, like land masses being in the same area, there are differences. We do not have the large oceans you do—we have no need for them to be as large, so they're smaller. Certain land masses are slightly different, as is some topography, but by and large the Earth plane is very similar to the Other Side. We do have what we call "quadrants" on the Other Side, which are nothing more than divided sections of the main continents—there are four for each, hence the name. You can read more about quadrants in some of Sylvia's other books.

I bring this up only because spirit guides tend to flock together in a quadrant that is in the area of Greece on your side. You may say, "But that's so far away!" unless you happen to be living in Greece, but time and space are irrelevant to us. We are seconds from anywhere or anyone. A blink of an eye would be more appropriate to describe the time it takes us to reach you in full essence.

A COG IN THE CIRCLE OF TIME

Now before I get into specifics of what a typical "day" for me would be like, let me emphasize that this very concept is rather difficult for me to understand. We don't really have time as you know it, for ours runs in a circle, while yours runs laterally. We don't designate time like you do, in minutes, hours, days, weeks, months, and so forth. I understand that it's useful for your finite mind, for you're used to the concept of time, but we do not deal with it on my side. You see, I would have to say "when I got up," for we do not sleep (or "get up" for that matter), and our circular time is very different in concept than yours, so it's very difficult to meld the two. With that in mind, let's pull out a cog in the circle of my time and designate it as the start of my day.

It's hard to say that a day in the life of a spirit guide is difficult, because we don't have days, seasons, or time. We don't have to sleep or eat or drink, yet we do have a body that's more organically and molecularly solid than any earthly body is. We're also all what you'd deem to be 30 years of age. No matter when we pass, we all become 30 very quickly when we reach the Other Side. When Sylvia asked me why this is, I said, "Because it is and always has been." Thirty seems to be the point of primary youth and maturity.

By the way, while we're talking about physical characteristics, no one on the Other Side has any deformities, and everyone has all their organs in perfectly healthy working condition—and there's no depression, vengeance, anger, or jealousy. Even though we keep our basic personalities over here, it's really the best of us—that is, without the human aggravations that cause our failings. Everyone has distinct looks, in all colors and sizes, but we're all beautiful and recognizable to each soul. As Sylvia says, "Souls recognize each other in any form, shape, or color."

Whether we guides are at the Council, listening to lectures, consulting master teachers or other guides, going to concerts, or what have you, we never, ever leave you unattended. Because we have full brain usage, we cannot only multitask, but we can be in several places at once and see and feel every facet of your life on all levels.

For instance, "today" I went to a very interesting lecture with many other guides. This lecture was about how time and distance condense, becoming faster than the speed of light. The speed of light can only be measured by what you think that speed is, but when it accelerates it naturally becomes quicker and evolves into a quantum leap. So I found this to be very interesting, even though unlike other guides, my forte is not the cosmology of things.

While I was attending the lecture, Sylvia was doing readings in her office for clients. She had gotten up a half hour later than usual (she is an early riser), and it put her off because she has a definite schedule about everything. In that way she's easy to track, but she always has so much going on. I am more on call than a guide who watches over a sedentary person. It has gotten easier as she has gotten older, but not much. I could go into a long litany of her drive and how she wore everyone out when she was younger, but that list would be too long.

To go on with my "day," another guide wanted me to listen to a lecture on astrophysics, so we went. I later went to a garden to meet with some other guides, many of whom wanted to discuss the lectures, but conversation as always turned to what was going on with the people we were guiding. Our focus is always on our charges.

Sylvia was finishing her readings, so she went out to eat with her son. They talked about a branch of Novus Spiritus opening in Canada, and she was excited. (This, strangely, is a little behind itself, but it's still on track and will catch up.) She went home and talked to me for a few minutes in her bedroom, and I told her that this was the first of three churches in Canada in the next year. She then spoke on the phone, took a bath, talked to Mother God, got out and dressed, watched the Discovery Channel for half an hour, and played with her dogs. (Her dogs see me, and I play with them, too.) Then she went in and wrote for two hours and went to bed. She never goes to sleep right away; she always worries about money for her corporation and the church. I tell her not to worry . . . to no avail. She finally went to sleep.

I then went into the Great Library and looked up some information on extraterrestrials that I have to talk to the ministers about next week in your time. When I came out, I could hear a concert going on in the distance, and I saw some people planting and gardening, while others were playing and talking to their animals, and still others were walking about in conversation. There is constant activity, along with ongoing research, travel, and movement over here. You never see anyone leaning against a tree sleeping—if their eyes are closed, they are meditating.

I also, as all guides do, go to the scanning orbs often, and this was my next stop. These are large glass orbs that show every part of a person's life in 3-D living color. This is also where a person comes as a part of orientation after they pass from life and come Home. We often check our charges' past lives as we have done before they wrote their charts, but we might reference a specific place or incident in this life or a past one that is causing a problem such as cell memory. This is where the soul carries over a fear or an aversion because of a past-life trauma. We see how it was dealt with and whether or not the experience was complete. If we see that it is still residing in the psyche or cells and is causing a problem in their present life, we then (as I mentioned earlier) try to push it to the surface so the person we are guiding can get rid of it.

You gave consent before you came down that your guide could scan a certain situation and how you handled it. If it is good, other guides will watch to advise their charges. So even if this makes you nervous, it shouldn't, because there is nothing in human behavior that we have not seen or that we don't understand. So you can imagine that you're in living color being scanned somewhere or the subject of some lecture or lectures that could be revealing in living color. Sylvia gave her permission to have us scan her life constantly, which is what I am doing now. When Sylvia started her church, we shared it many times because it was so important—the persistence and dedication to one person's beliefs against all odds *[okay, that's enough]* was viewed by many.

Before you incarnated, we went over your charts with you time and time again, and even questioned you on whether you wanted to take this or that trauma—yet you are usually adamant to get it over with, finish it, and learn for God. It is not wrong for us, humanized as we are, to be proud of our charges and even feel sadness when they fail, although it may be in their chart to do so. We may know the ending, but the process to get there is hard to watch and guide . . . which is why we are so fortunate to have the Council and God to help us.

So, I entered a vast auditorium and saw many guides sitting at the scanning orbs. Although we know the chart of the people we are guiding, we never stop researching or getting advice from various sources on every facet of our charges' lives. We are aware that perhaps a tragedy is coming, such as the death of a child or a devastating illness, and we are constantly looking for ways to help you through this part of your life. As silent as it may seem to you, we do give comfort. The quieter you are, even in your darkest moments, the more we can get in and call in God and His and Her forces to help you get through life.

You must also keep in mind that all of life is a learning process—even the most despotic acts can be humorous. I don't mean cruelty, but some things you do can be a form of not only human behavior but of our learning to deal with you and your chart. Let's say it is an inventory of human knowledge or of human behavior and what we can do. We certainly have reviewed our own lives and also learn from you as you learn from us. Great lectures are done on the whole scenarios of lives or a life, and strangely enough, it can be done before you come Home.

Part of the test of life in an incarnate state is the lack of the full utilization of your brain, for knowledge of not only the Other Side, but Father and Mother God, too—and the real truth of things as they really are is only available with full brain capacity. The only way to increase your brainpower while in life is through spirituality, but you cannot attain your full capacity on the Earth plane no matter what you do . . . it is not meant for that plane of existence. You might even liken it to the evolvement of the soul: The more evolved your soul becomes in life, the more your brain can utilize its God-given power, and when you pass over, your soul magnifies itself and the power of the brain follows to full utilization. To oversimplify, negativity restricts brainpower and the blossoming of the soul.

Our minds on the Other Side are much more capable of utilizing power than yours because we use the total brainpower available and you do not. Your minds are finite in that only a segment of your brain capability is utilized. There is a reason for this, for you are in an incarnate state on a negative plane of existence and "away at school," so to speak. When you come Home, your brain opens up to full capacity, and the use of your entire brain becomes a reality.

It is very hard in the human body to remember that you or your loved ones who die are going Home. In fact, it is a great contrivance not to let you remember too much, because if you did, as Sylvia says, everyone would be jumping off bridges instead of going through life on Earth again. I liken it to the pain of childbirth: We forget it until we have another child and the pain starts. Then it all comes back with a rush, but unfortunately there is no turning back.

The worst part is that we forget the pain of life very easily before we incarnate. We also forget how long or short time can be. But you must remember that the Other Side is your Home . . . you have always existed here and you always will be here.

CHAPTER 12

INTERVIEW WITH A SPIRIT GUIDE

The following is an excerpt from a research trance session in which Francine was asked questions about what she does on the Other Side and about the concept of time. Some of this may seem a little redundant, but it bears repeating because it shows how interested the ministers are in Francine's knowledge and what she does in her "job" as my guide. For the sake of clarity, the questions asked of Francine are in italics.

You don't have time on the Other Side.

No, we do not.

We're time-bound, while you have . . . let's call it "duration." You engage in conversation, right?

Oh yes.

We experience duration differently, depending on our psychological state—if we're having a great time, it's over quickly; but if we're miserable, things just seem to drag on.

But you don't understand, it's because you are time-bound that you experience this. Without time, there is constant duration—we have no deadlines. Well, we do know that we would like to see this lecture, but if we don't catch it, it will come again. And the one thing that we find with people who come over is that the hardest orientation for them is to know that there is time for everything.

You don't have to watch the clock.

No. We don't have a dinner hour, we don't have people coming home for something, we don't have to be at a certain place at a certain time. If we want to amble over to a lecture, we do. If we've missed it, we can always catch it on the scanner, or it will return again.

Okay, you have a sense of the linear time, in that if you miss a lecture, you could just go back 15 minutes, in some sense, and pick up the lecture where it started?

No, I wouldn't have to, because everything is rotating in a circle.

What is your experience of duration, and how does that coincide with your being in Sylvia now and then?

I have had to become time-bound; I also had to learn very early that I couldn't contact her at four in her morning because she got very aggravated with that.

So is there a part of you that's monitoring Sylvia as you're wandering about on the Other Side?

Of course. I can see when she is sleeping, and I can see when she is lying in a prone position and her eyes are closed. I can also see when she is more open, because I have been with her so long. All of your guides can see that. We are—or at least we try to be—diplomatic and tactful about your life.

So when she needs you, how do you get that recall notice?

Well, I'm always with her.

You're also off in the garden and at the lecture . . .

We always have a visual of the person we're with. Let me give you an example: How many times can a mother be talking to someone, but she's always got that inner eye on her child? She always has that sixth sense of her child even if she is not there.

It's like a psychic link?

It is a psychic link, but it is also a sensory link.

Sylvia gets up at around 7 A.M. Where were you?

I was in a lecture.

So when did you next come back and visit her?

I was with her at the lecture.

What were you doing when Sylvia was having lunch?

I was in a garden.

So how much did you do between her waking and the garden?

It all blends. It was all very quick to me, just as your time is very quick to all of us here—80 years in your time is like weeks to us. The only thing that helps us guides is the fact that we're more slowed down, otherwise we would blink and it would be all over. You see, you want time to bind us, and it cannot. You have the seasons and you get old and you die—we don't. Time takes its toll on you, and we don't have that because we have no "time" in your sense of the word.

Realizing that we're time-bound and you're not, when you're tracking us, you're not looking at time and space as being two separate entities?

That's right. We're just watching a fish in a big ocean, that's all . . . and we don't really know what the point of the ocean is—we don't have a reference point.

So as guides you're just stepping in and tuning in to us using our time as a point of reference, not yours?

Yes. The only way we can track it is within your time framework, but it means nothing to us. The cosmology of your time is quite ridiculous to us, even though we all lived in it when we were in life. We find it to be amazingly archaic . . . yet we know that it has to be.

So the only thing in our time that has slowed light to the speed that we think it is are our restricted minds, and in reality it's instantaneous?

Yes, and the only way we can relate to that is to become somewhat humanized so that we get into your time framework, or else we wouldn't care.

So you almost have to isolate yourself from your own dimensional perspective to get into ours to view it, right?

All of us can view without isolation, but guides have to isolate themselves and descend into your dimension to become more humanized.

So on the Other Side, you know that there are all these things you want to study and research, and you just do it, as opposed to our side where we worry, "I'm this age . . . what am I supposed to be learning and doing?"

That's right. And you always ask yourself, "Oh my God, have I missed it?" "Am I too old for school?" "Do I want to start a family—how much time do I have for that?" and "How much time do I have before I retire?" And it's all mass confusion and hysteria. Your time is your stress is what I'm saying—it's so stressful. If you had time removed from you, I promise that you would have 98 percent of your anxiety taken away.

Could you address the fact of interdimensional causation, such as how much the negativity on this plane affects yours, or how much the positive energy on your plane affects ours?

The positive energy on our plane infringes on you tremendously; the negativity of your plane does not bother us. The only way negativity bothers us is in being a guide and in being humanized to perform that function. There is no negativity on my side, but because guides become humanized to have a certain empathy and understanding of their charges, they sometimes absorb some negativity when their charges go through tremendous trauma or pain. Guides who become over-loaded with negativity and pain from watching what their charges have to go through go into a cleansing type of therapy on my side to stay at maximum functioning level. I have gone through this myself when Sylvia was enduring so much emotion or pain. This keeps us guides at our maximum efficiency level.

In Sylvia's Journey of the Soul books, they talk about us being a spark of the Divine, and then when we're about two years old, this veil of ignorance or forgetfulness comes over us . . . Can you explain that further?

Yes. Let me explain it to you like this. You have all been trained on our side to be, for lack of a better word, *survivalists*. You have been trained to come down to the dark shadow lands, which is Earth. You've been helped by the Council, you've been talked to by guides and angels, and that is all in the morphic resonance of your being. But part of that training or knowledge is going to be forgotten, just like when you take subjects in school and forget part of the teaching later on in life. So we have to almost put it in your limbic brain as the instinctual knowledge to survive. That's why it's so harsh to commit suicide, because that's defying the instinctual programming of survival and completing your chart for God.

Just before you enter into an incarnation, we tell you that you'll be brainwashed by the world, but something in your soul will rise up to survive. The more spiritual you become, the more you'll rise up again and again, and the more things will be made clearer. Don't you see what that is? That's stripping away all the worldly things of this planet so that you become pure spirit again; but the only way you can become pure spirit is to come down into the shadow lands through incarnations. And each time there's a layer that's peeled away until you do become more evolved and become pure spirit, and that's what everyone is aspiring to.

One of the Journey books talks about time, and struggling with trying to explain it because our world is so time-based.

You can't do it, you can't explain it, because the minute you say, "But wait a minute," you've already lost it. So if you look, and I know it's very difficult, but if you look at a circle and don't see yourself in it, but pull yourself out of it and then look back at the circle and say, "That is the Now"—we are all in the Now of God. And the Now only means (it's not that esoteric) that there is no time, everything happens in the Now. To try to understand time from a timelessness is impossible—except that it always rotates, it's always there, there's always enough lateral movement to get everything done that you want—because if you say, "There is enough time to get everything done that you want," you've lost the concept again.

You said that if you missed a lecture, you would catch it when it came back. Can you say how long that would be?

No. We would just know that whenever we wanted it to be, it would be available.

When just one person wanted it to be?

Oh yes, because, you see, with time going in a circle, you can pick it up.

What I heard you implying was that you can just get the lecturer to redo the lecture.

No, I did not say that, I never said that. I said, "We could pick it up." If a person is in a regression, their mind travels back in time. For example, they might go back to when they were a child or go into a past life. All of those experiences would be in a short period of time on your plane—they might be living a lifetime in an hour, yet they are still themselves in this time and place. At any time the person can back up and pick a life up because the mind and soul are moving, and yet—are they not usually in a stationary position while doing this?

So basically we should take the word time out of it and instead say "sequences that are not relevant to a directional flow"?

That's right. I think that Sylvia's analogy of a record, which was a stroke of genius, says it best. She said that the Now is like a needle on a phonograph record that keeps moving from groove to groove, and yet it's the same record.

You're standing on the Other Side, you missed the lecture, but it will come around again—where do you go for this to happen?

For lack of a better terminology, I can jump a groove, or if you want to make it very simplistic, let's say I can walk or go backward.

Would it be akin to dipping into the Akashic Records?

It's always there. Aren't all your lives always there; are you not living all your lives as real as you feel you are living your life now? This becomes evident when you are put into regression, and it depends on how deep you go.

We're trying to equate the physical motion to the—

No, not physical motion, you're talking about *soul* motion. You're in a physical body that needs glasses, you have to go to the bathroom, you have to eat, you have to put on clothes, you have to bathe, and you have a thousand time-limiting things.

The reason that's very significant is because we define time as a change of motion, what we call the "atomic clock." So yes, you're right—we're physical, we base time on physical movement, but you don't.

If a holy man is up on a mountain sitting cross-legged and there are no seasonal changes, he will have a sense of time, but not as much as you would by experiencing those changes. That's what the ancient hermits or supposed holy men did to try to find a deeper meaning . . . although I agree with Sylvia in that it's a waste of a life to sit there and hope to find some deeper meaning when the whole purpose of life is to become a person of motion, do good, and help others.

It seems that our bodies are what make us time-bound.

Yes, but there's a reason for that. It is for survival on your plane. But our life is so full of joy on my side. You may not think that lectures, study, and research are joyful, but gaining knowledge really is. Then of course, we guides will go see the Council, our Brotherhood of One, where we converse with master teachers and gain tremendous love knowledge; or we'll go to the Towers for a while; or we'll go to other planets and visit our friends, and in the process be fed endless amounts of knowledge constantly. And you can always notice on my side when somebody has gotten a great amount of knowledge, or as we say, "the gulp of knowledge," for they just seem to shimmer more. We can feel them just shimmering with it in a state of euphoria. It's like an epiphany, a mental orgasmic feeling that brings the greatest of happiness and joy.

Now I realize that you may not be able to relate to this type of joy on your plane, for you have a physical body that feels pleasure in your sexual act, or in playing a game of baseball, or riding a surfboard, or any number of physical acts that bring pleasure. But really think about life and what brings joy: seeing the first steps of your child, the euphoria of being in love, a puppy hopping like a bunny, a gorgeous sunrise or sunset, a loving smile being given to you, beautiful memories, the joy of discovery, the feeling of elation and happiness when you've done a good deed, reading a good book, gaining knowledge . . . all of these interact with the mind and emotions, more so than with the physical body. Then multiply that a thousandfold, and you might start to understand the joy we have on the Other Side.

When we study the Journey books, time is said to be related in certain points as sequencing life after life after life, yet you can have them all at any time and pick them up. It's like seeing that something is happening in a row, yet it's not happening that way—sequencing itself but not sequencing itself . . . it seems so jumbled.

It's not, though—your record is a small circle within a huge circle. Please think of it as if everyone has a little record inside a larger record, and those records are all revolving at the same time. Don't ever think it's jumbled, because it's very self-contained. Your record is individual from anyone else, like your fingerprints or your DNA—it is individually yours, and it may only mean something to you, although other people can access it if you allow them to. But along with all these millions of little records is the giant record, which of course is Mother and Father God. So it's not jumbled, it's very itemized, and it's replete with specific knowledge . . . there's nothing more perfected than that.

All of our lives are concurrently going on (and that in itself is mind-boggling), but the realization has to come that you don't have that privileged viewpoint— God has it. So from our perspective, we're only living our life as we know it now . . . the dang needle is right here, right now.

Oh yes, you're full essence. Some years ago we had a discussion in one of these classes and someone had challenged Raheim, who was doing a trance in Sylvia's body for research purposes. Now Raheim is not the best person to challenge, for his knowledge is vast, but the challenge came in the form that this person believed that only part of our essence is here, but the rest of it was scattered throughout all these ribbons of time. And Raheim very definitely said, "No, full essence is here, but the other essences that you can pick up are in God's Now." I know that might seem more complicated, but you can access it. Very much like if you were to watch a movie of, let's say, when you were born in this life; or you go back and your mother shows you pictures of you and your first tricycle, and you say, "Oh, now I remember that." You're sort of living again, in some minute way, that little child who was—and that's how you do it here.

Keep in mind that when you come to our side, if you want to go back and access a particular period of time, you can. At one point, for instance, Raheim was doing some research and got caught in a Mongolian war. I mean he went into the Akashic Records and actually got caught in a physical stampede. It didn't hurt him, but it must have been frightening, because once you open that door into those records, everything is there, which makes it very divinely wondrous. If we want to go back to the time of Merlin and King Arthur (who were real people, by the way) or the time of the Crusades, we can. We can't assume a persona unless we actually were that persona in a past life, but we can go back as almost a spirit that is observing and viewing and actually experience the time and place with all its emotion.

What's the difference between going into the Akashic Records and the Hall of Wisdom?

When you go into the Akashic Records, you actually experience the time and place, with all its smells, emotion, violence, and so forth, even though you are generally an observer in spirit form. However, when you go to the Hall of Wisdom, you can read it or view it on a scanner, but you cannot experience it in totality. It would be much like if you went to a movie and you were watching it (Hall of Wisdom), but then all of a sudden one of the characters in the movie pulled you into the movie itself so that you are now participating in it (Akashic Records).

Francine, you indicated that you often take notes at lectures—do you retain everything from such learning experiences?

Absolutely. I take mental notes of something that is important, but in actuality, I retain everything. You on your Earth plane only retain about 15 percent of what you learn through your life, which I know you might find somewhat depressing. We, on the other hand, retain 100 percent of what we learn, and it is ingrained in our souls.

Is it correct to say that in the elimination of time and space, that's when you have total control of yourself?

Yes. You on your plane are controlled by your atmosphere, your time, your jobs, your keeping your body clean, your habits, your eating, your sleeping—you are not in control of anything. I think that is why Sylvia says that when you're in the body, you're out of control. It is the aging process, it is the coming into life, it is the bravest of the brave, it is total surrender . . . that is why survival of life is such a feat. While we are in spirit, we are in total control: We can go anywhere we want, we can do anything we want, we're not bound by time and space, we're not bound by sickness or hunger or tiredness, we're not bound by clothes or by having to fix ourselves up—none of that is necessary on my side.

By the usage of the term spirit, *do you mean that we won't have a body on the Other Side?*

Absolutely not. We do have bodies that are more real and solid than yours because we are in the framework of reality. You are in a temporary plane of existence, while we are in the timeless place of reality where we all exist forever. Our bodies are a manifestation of a portion of our spirit that is magnified in the close presence of God. Our spirit (or soul, if you will) is our real self, and it exists in our real home, the Other Side.

When we come to the Other Side, we will want to see you, Raheim, Jesus, and so on. I'm sure we all feel that way very strongly. When we get there and want to visit with Christ, will he have people meeting us, or how does it work?

No, Jesus will not have people meeting you, but he has a tremendous ability to be in several places at one time in variables that are far more extensive than we know. We know that in essence he can bilocate, trilocate, or take as many forms as necessary.

But you would be surprised at the people who don't want to see him right away. We find that to be quite amazing. We find that people don't ever think that it's possible until somebody does the nudge number and says, "Don't you want to see Christ or Azna?" "Don't you want to see the Father, don't you want to see people?" It never dawns on them that it is available to them.

When you're in Sylvia's body, Francine, are you here in full essence or are you bilocating?

Oh no, I'm here in full essence. I would never, ever go into her in half essence. I would be afraid that she would die. I have to manipulate her body—I have to at least keep her breathing and whatever else needs to be done.

So what is Sylvia doing right now?

Sitting on a park bench over here . . . just sitting there.

It sounds like she is very quiet, almost like there is no time passing. What is that feeling when everything gets really quiet and you almost feel like time has stopped?

Oh yes, all of a sudden it gets very quiet and it's like life is in slow motion. That's how it feels right before you die: It gets very euphoric and very quiet and very elongated—all of a sudden you get a touch of *I have infinity now*, and that's the beauty of it. That's the first thing you're aware of—it's not just the light, but that stretch of infinity . . . that "ahhhh". . . that letting go of all that harassment and the harried feeling and the body aches that you weren't even aware of, and it's just euphoric.

Is there a main thing that most of us come over with when we do pass? Do we want to say it's like "I would have, I should have, and I could have"?

I think everyone comes over with the "I should have, I could have, I didn't" for just a very short period of time, because for some reason we find you trailing time behind you. We find that when you come over to our side, right away you have a tendency to rush around and want to do everything. The first things people say are, "Do I have to sleep . . . are you sure I don't have to?" or "Do I have to rest?" or "I want to see my friends or my animals." We have to go, "Shhh, you have all the time you need."

Speaking of animals, you said that they're only here on Earth once, but there are too many animals now that are going to the light. Where do they all go?

There is plenty of room on my side. There are approximately six billion people on your planet now, and there are almost twice that many that were made for this planet—and the same is true of animals. Just as we do not have time to limit us, neither do we have space, so there's plenty of room for billions of animals.

You mentioned that our family members would be waiting for us. Did you mean from this life or also other lives?

Oh, all lives. And all the animals and all the people that you have known and loved and all the friends on the Other Side that never incarnated with you. That's a lot. A point of interest here is that on my side, you can understand what an animal says . . . they talk to us and they can also understand us.

I must go now.

Thank you, Francine.

AFTERWORD

When I began to write the new section for this book, I had feelings of elation and even a kind of "homesick sadness," like a long-forgotten memory that stirs in your soul and brings back a morphic resonance of what was, and will be again. I felt somewhat the same way when I was writing *The Other Side and Back* and the *Journey of the Soul* series.

Yet this had a different flavor, like I was scanning my life with an old friend. You see, I know Francine so well, but I also got many revelations hearing about her days with me. I also began to have a renewed appreciation for her. Even though she didn't complain, I could feel the pathos and the humor and even the helplessness she felt at times. After all, as she states, spirit guides have to become more humanized to understand us. So even though they're on the Other Side, a lot of the bliss is taken away when you're a guide or they wouldn't be able to care about us.

I began to see that guides are in a type of seclusion. I mean, yes, they can attend lectures and festivals, but they're always on call. So unlike the other entities around them, spirit guides really aren't free, but it's also their way of perfecting for God from their side.

I remember when my father was very ill and I was so afraid to ask Francine if his light was blinking (when a soul is coming over, they have a light that blinks like on a huge tote board to let everyone know that they're coming Home—this way, they can gather to meet the soul who's coming over). With an even more high-pitched voice than normal, which I swear had a slight tremor to it, Francine said yes. Why didn't *I* know?

I really did, but I hoped I was wrong. Remember, we mediums are never psychic about ourselves and our loved ones. When you love someone, many times you'd rather take the pain than have them go through it.

I remember one dark night when I cried out to Francine, "I wish it was you going through this and not me!" The next words I heard were, "So do I." I felt so bad and so selfish that I never said it again. After all, I chose this chart . . . granted, when we're going through a difficult time, that's not much consolation.

I happened to catch a show on TV the other night about women going through plastic surgery, and afterward they were crying from the pain and asking themselves why they ever consented to it. One woman even said, "I bit off more than I could chew." Well, two months later they looked in the mirror and guess what? They were beautiful, and all the pain was forgotten. In fact, everyone said after the fact that they'd do it again. I thought about how that's just like life. Spirit guides know that the end result will be all right, but the souls that they're guiding have to go through the process of their own spiritual growth.

Our guides are our friends and kindred souls, and they know more about us than we do—and if we fall, they try to pick us up. I once asked Francine if she ever felt a sense of failure, and she said, "Not about you so much, but about the fact that I couldn't do more." She also said that many guides are surprised by the things they think we'll take badly, while at other times, things that they feel are not that traumatic are devastating to us. It doesn't mean that we're goofy or off-chart, it's just that we're human, so sometimes stress levels, hormones, or so forth set us off.

More than any doctor, paramedic, or counselor, our guides are trained to handle almost any and all situations. Francine says that sometimes just holding the white light of the Holy Spirit around us and calling in extra help from angels and God really helps. Our guides aren't necessarily more powerful than angels, but they certainly are the head administrators of our lives. They'll call in healers, angels, the Council—anyone and everyone who they feel will help. So allow them into your mind and heart because they're the guardians of our lives down here. They truly are the finger of God.

I think it's a wonderful idea for you to keep a journal. In the evening, write down all of the events, big or small, that seem to be beyond coincidence. You may be surprised by the questions you come up with, such as, "Why did I do that? Why did I say that? What made me have that reaction?"

Many times my clients tell me things they've said or done that were seemingly out of character. But were they really? Or was there an infused message from their spirit guide? Sometimes it's only later that we realize we were right about a situation or a person that at the time we had no conscious knowledge of.

I'm very avid about diary or journal writing because it accomplishes many things. Obviously it allows you to remember events, but it also enables you to recognize definite patterns. It helps to imprint your consciousness with the knowledge that something is definitely going on outside of yourself. It also tells the guides that you're trying to pierce the spiritual veil to make them accessible to us.

Listen for them to call your name. Hear that voice in your head and heart—it's always there if you're just quiet and let it in. Try to be neutral and let them send you messages, even though I know that it's hard to leave out what you want and discern what's real. As I've said so many times and in so many ways, you don't have to believe, but the rationale is that God doesn't leave us down here without help, love, and guidance. Even if you don't believe, leave your mind open to explore, and like our Lord said, "Seek and ye shall find." I know that you'll find logical truth in a world that's sometimes filled with chaos, and to know that God loves and protects you and sends emissaries to keep you is a wondrous gift.

There are no secrets from a guide, yet they love us anyway—that's very comforting to me. They know our human foibles because they've also lived before. In their conferring with other guides, I'm sure there isn't anything they haven't heard or seen (and after 51 years of readings, I often feel the same way). Guides talk incessantly to each other, but there's also a very strong code of ethics. I've never heard Francine say, "Boy, do I have a story to tell you about what so-and-so is doing." But she will give me warnings if my staff or friends are getting into what we might call a "danger zone."

Many of my clients have seen Francine in their dreams because she's so well known, and she'll come if she's called (which they all do). Does she mind? Of course not. You can even send your guides to someone to bring grace and healing or even help them cross over. All guides can help other guides.

They're probably the unsung heroes of this planet, but they don't have the ego to mind. It's their job, and they do it with love, patience, and finesse. Through it all, to the end of our days, they stand with us to the right side (people have actually seen Francine when I was lecturing, long before she was ever described), never wavering and always in a state of protection and love.

Our guides are never bothered with jealousy, vengeance, pettiness, sarcasm, or being mean-spirited; but they certainly, as we do, have their own personalities. I thought many years ago that Francine was kind of stuffy and rigid, but I've since grown to understand that she had to be a no-nonsense person. After all, who'd want a giddy, silly guide? (Although with some of the people I've read for, you wonder!)

So, when you're at your lowest point and think that no one is around, remember that spirit guides are there helping, petitioning, and giving solace. If you keep your mind quiet and ask a question, you may be surprised that an answer comes through if you just stop obsessing for a few minutes to let them in. They're the truest friends you will ever have on this earth, with nothing on their mind except your well-being. (But they're never meant to take the place of Mother and Father God.) So please don't feel alone.

God bless our spirit guides . . . and thank You, God, for allowing them to help us through this sometimes hellish arena that we call life.

EXERCISES FOR RECEIVING MESSAGES

The exercises that follow will help you open up your psyche to a greater extent, enabling you to better receive messages from your spirit guide(s).

EXERCISE 1

This short exercise really helps get the mind ready to receive messages, and it only takes a few minutes. Let's call this our "training exercise."

In your mind, take yourself to a seashore, and put your back against a palm tree. Place your feet in the warm sand. Feel the sun on your face, the breeze in your hair. You can make this as simple or as intricate as you wish. Look up at the clouds and take three deep breaths, feeling all the negativity and hurt flowing out of you, down through your whole body, and out your toes into the gentle waves that are lapping against your feet. Then out of the shadows from the palm trees, ask your guide to come to you. Ask a simple question. Even ask their name. As time progresses, don't be afraid to ask the guide specific questions that you can later validate.

EXERCISE 2

This exercise flexes the so-called psychic muscle, getting your mind ready to receive messages.

Lie in a prone position. Visualize the white light of the Holy Spirit around you. Feel that a green light of healing surrounds the white light, then put a purple light of high spirituality around that. You are now relaxed, feeling that all illness and stress is leaving. Your mind and body are quiet, yet rejuvenated. Your soul is expanding with each beat of your heart.

You see yourself inside a beautiful room. The lights in the room keep changing colors from white to green to purple. All of a sudden, you are aware that there is a presence that has come up behind you. You are not afraid. In this expanded awareness, you have the sense that this is a presence you know and recognize. You do not have to see the visage right away, but you know this entity. This is your spirit guide, someone whom you love and have loved and trusted your entire life. See if the guide will give you an audible message or even a telepathic one. Let yourself lie there relaxed. Then come back to consciousness, feeling absolutely wonderful.

Sometimes this is a good way to drift off to sleep. You may even awaken with a firm imprint of a message.

EXERCISE 3

I've used this meditation before in other books, but it bears repeating. This is what I call an "active meditation."

Find a quiet place in your home. Get a chair and place it in the middle of the space. Now place a white candle to the left of the chair, a white candle to the right, a white candle in front, and another in back of the chair. Light the candles and then sit in the chair. You're surrounded by lights that not only protect, but also attract the guides. Sit quietly and ask for your guide to cross over this circle of light and give you a sign. You may feel a feathery breeze or gentle touch on your cheek or hair. Again, ask a question and see if you get an answer. Stay in the circle for 15 to 20 minutes, relaxing, breathing deeply, and talking to your guide. Then get up, blow out the candles, and feel rejuvenated.

(*Please note*: Never let candles burn all night, and always use containers that are flameproof to prevent fires.)

EXERCISE 4

This is another good exercise to help you open up as much as possible.

Take a deep breath and relax your whole body, from your feet, ankles, thighs, and pelvic area, all the way up through the trunk of your body; and up the neck, shoulders, upper and lower arms, hands, and fingertips. Come up to the neck, the face, around the mouth, the nose, and the eyes.

Now see yourself in a beautiful green meadow. There are flowers around you. You feel so free and so alive. You're aware that you're wearing a robe that's loose-fitting and flowing. Your feet are bare. As you run or walk or float through this meadow, you're suddenly aware that right in front of you appears a golden door. You pull the door open effortlessly, and you see white steps leading upward. You climb up about six steps and find yourself on a beautiful white marble platform. There's a purple mist around you. In the middle of this mist is the beautiful entity that is your guide. The guide comes toward you and embraces you. You feel so much love, peace, and healing. You descend the steps, and the guide comes with you. You open the door and run back across the meadow. You now come back to yourself with a feeling of protection and unconditional love, and you're more empowered inside than you have ever been.

You can use any or all of the meditative exercises in this chapter. The more you use them, the more you're becoming predisposed to not only hearing or even having a sense of a presence, but also to receiving valid messages. The guides who know us better than we know ourselves are aware that we're "stretching" to get in touch with them. They, in turn, will stretch toward us, and together, this synergy will make it easier for the guides to contact us. Once the veil of belief is opened, the knowledge is immeasurable, and your life will be forever enriched by the loving guide who has been assigned to help you along the path of life.

SPIRIT GUIDE MEDITATION: INTRODUCTION AND TRANSCRIPT

INTRODUCTION

On the free audio download that accompanies this book, I answer some questions about spirit guides, such as: *Does everyone have a spirit guide? Where do spirit guides come from? How do we know if we are receiving messages from our guides—or just imagining things?* Drawing on my personal experience and the knowledge imparted by Francine, I share the truth about these mystical beings with you.

I go on to illuminate the difference between angels and spirit guides, reveal techniques for better communication with them, and unveil the process that these guides must go through before they're able to help each and every one of us.

If you've ever wanted to understand more about the mysterious world of angels and spirits, I hope that this introduction will provide the answers you're looking for. As always, please remember that you're never really alone. You're surrounded by those who want to aid and protect you—and you have the power to ask for their help!

> The meditation included in the download can help each one of you find out who your spirit guide is and how to maintain contact with him or her.

TRANSCRIPT OF "SPIRIT GUIDE MEDITATION"

[Editor's Note: We have included the verbatim text of the "Spirit Guide Meditation" here (which you can download by following the instructions on page x and is excerpted from one of Sylvia's lectures) in case you'd like to follow along or would like to refer back to it at a later date.]

Okay. So sit up straight, put your feet flat on the floor [Pause], and it would be really nice if you just kind of put your hands in your lap with your palms upward. That's sort of like a way of receiving grace. And I want you to put a white light of the Holy Spirit around you. [Pause] And I want you to feel this descending of peace, harmony, quiet, and God-centeredness, Christ's consciousness that's always with us, Mother and Father God, and the love that Mother and Father God have for each other creates the Holy Spirit.

And you can put anyone else in there you wish. You can put Bahá'u'lláh [founder of the Bahá'í religion], you can put Buddha; in fact, you can stack 'em. I'd call on *all* of them to attend you. And I want you to feel yourself very relaxed. And you'll get adept enough that you can even give yourself a code-color word—let's just use the word *blue*—which means that from this point on, that whenever you say it to yourself, you'll be right back into this lucid, meditative, *valid knowledge* of where you're going and what you're going to see.

And I want you to relax your toes, your instep, almost like you're *un*-stressing. Your ankles, your calves, your knees, your thighs, the whole pelvic girdle, up through the trunk, down through the shoulders, the upper arms, the lower arms, the hands, the fingertips. Up through the neck. Around the face, the mouth, the nose, the eyes, and the forehead.

And let's even go behind the eyes now. Almost like we can make it [the mind] escape, like so much dark smoke, not necessarily a blank, but a peaceful, quiet [**Pause**] vacuum. Not a vacuum in which knowledge doesn't come through, but also very much like the monks, who, by the way, shave the top of their head, their tonsures, because they felt that they could be infused better without hair on the top of their head. But let's say, "My opening in the top of my head, from my pineal to my hypothalamus, to my pituitary, is open, so that I can infuse and bring knowledge in." Not random knowledge—we don't want to know that all the flotsam and jetsam in the world's gonna filter in, that we can do anything about—but put a codicil on it. In other words, only, dear God, what I can help with, adapt to, give warnings for. This also increases your psychic ability.

Now, I want you to *visualize* yourself in a meadow. And if you can't visualize it, sense it. And the meadow is very green. And all of a sudden, you're very aware that you are in light-fitting clothes. If you're a male, you are in a long robe like our Lord used to wear; if you're a female, then you can be in a gossamer robe, anything that's free-moving. You look down, and you see, in front of you, *white*. Brilliant white flag-stone steps. They're not going upward, they're leading across this beautiful green meadow. With great antici-pation, you begin to hop these stones. And they begin to wind around through this meadow. And you feel the sun in your face, warm, the wind in your hair, and you keep jumping the stones.

And all of a sudden, in the middle of this meadow, you see this beautiful, white, gleaming gazebo. It seems to be strangely not out of place, but it's just there. And there's something familiar about it, like almost that you were running ahead and you knew that you were gonna come upon something that was that beautiful. Shining, bright, brilliant. And you run up to this gazebo, and there's three steps leading up. But you don't really go up those steps; you stand there for a moment. And out of the shadows of the gazebo [Pause] steps a figure that appears at the top of the step. Take your first impression. Do not let *imagination*, the word, come in, the creation of your own mind. Let it be. This entity—tall, short, medium, whatever it might be—begins to descend the steps. And there is such a marvelous sense of, like we said yesterday, *Oh, there you are.* A familiarity, a feeling of positive energy, a feeling of love.

This person has descended the steps, puts their arm around you. You say to this person, "What is your name?"

Now, please don't be discouraged if it happens to be a loved one. Because a loved one can have, sometimes, priority, and *push* the person, or the guide out of the way, and show up as William or Ed or whoever it might be. Don't push anyone away, because whoever's the most prominent, or whoever you need, might show up. Your spouse who's passed . . . but many times it's a guide. Go with the first impression of the name. Even if it's not spoken—so much of this is telepathic.

Now with the guide's arms around you, embracing, you walk down the path again. The white flagstone steps. And right when you get about to the middle, before you get to the end, I want you to turn to the guide, and ask them any question that you don't know the answer to that you would have to validate. Please do not be concerned that they would be upset that you have to validate this. Even if you want to ask a question about, "How long will it be before my finances . . ." Don't expect a long verbiage right yet, especially if you haven't met them before. Say, "Give me a time in which my finances will be better," " . . . that I'll find someone . . ." and take the first impression. If it's two years, six months, three weeks, take your first impression.

And you continue down the flagstone steps until you come back to where you started.

Now, because you're going to come back to yourself, you leave your guide there, but that doesn't mean your guide is there, because you're just coming back to yourself, in your own dimension. But the guide stays right next to you. You've just gone on a higher plane to meet your guide is all. But before you come back to yourself, you turn to the right, away from the flagstone steps, and all of a sudden, you walk a few feet and you see right in front of you, huge brass doors that seem to be just standing upright. Curiosity is a marvelous thing, and they have big rings on them, the doors, and they look heavy. But you take one of the rings and you pull it and, by God, if it doesn't just swing open. And you look down this long hallway.

You're barefooted, as I stated. And you find yourself entering this long hallway. And you're aware that pink marble on the floor under your feet is very cool. Still wearing the same loose clothing. And you run with anticipation. Even if you feel in this life you can't run. Boy, are you running now. Because the spirit can run.

And all of a sudden, you come to another set of doors, very much like the first, not as large, and you swing them open with no effort. All of a sudden, you're in a round room bathed in pink light. Pink light, of course, is always love. Pink is always love. Very pink. And all of a sudden, you, I mean your eyes, become accustomed to the pinkness of the room. Everything stands out in great relief. You look ahead of you and there looks like it's an altar stone. Like what priests stand behind, or now they stand in front of—and you find yourself circling this room and its heavy draped, pink drapes.

Something pulls you to this altar stone. You run your hand, for some reason, under the altar stone, and your finger hits something that's metal, and you realize it's a key. Now you run your hand over the top of the marble, and there's a keyhole. You put the gold key in the keyhole and you turn it, and all of a sudden, the curtains part. And out of the curtains, almost like a stage, your guide steps. And I bet you anything, it's the same form, or sex, or personage, or sense of male or female—that might be all you get at the beginning, which is enough. And they guide you to another part of the room that also has curtains. And they open. And the guide directs you almost telepathically to ask any question you wish.

Now here's what we're gonna do. This is when we're going higher up, just like that lovely lady asked me, "Is it from my guide, is it from God?" Because we have to have things, we can't just be nebulous. Eventually, you will be. But you've got to have the exercises. All of a sudden, a golden scroll drops. Beautiful golden, brilliant. Almost like you'd think of something that was written, like the Ten Commandments. And your guide is sort of telepathically saying, "Ask God." You stand in front of this, almost like a sacred scroll, and you say, "Dear God, I want to know, dada-dada-da," whatever. [Pause] And all of a sudden, words begin to form: "How is my health?" "How are my finances going to be?" "What can I do to avoid anything that is health related?" "What should I do about my family?" You might get even the words *come*, *go forward more*, or *back off.* Even that, in itself, is an answer.

The guide has their arm around you, and now this is a room also in which you can find your loved ones, because they begin to congregate. Also, so do angels, because it's like a tabernacle. Because of the altar stone, you can make it as beautiful as you want. You can have it with a crucifix, you can have it with a statue, or you can have it just plain. But showing you two ways that you can infuse, eventually you won't need a scroll, you won't need the guide to lead you, but we have to take these steps to get there. Now you turn around, and the guide leads you to the door. Down the marble hallway, the guide is walking with you. You're laughing, you're talking, and you can also ask them something. "How 'bout my depression?" "How 'bout my marriage?" "How 'bout my health?" "How 'bout my children?" And wait for an answer. It might be very short, succinct, to the point—that's fine. Later on, if you keep doing it, it'll get more elaborate.

Come all the way back through the doors. You've already come through the one set of doors, now you're going through the big doors. All of a sudden, you find yourself now—it's almost like a kaleidoscope—at a seashore. Oh my! It's so warm and beautiful, the sand is white. You dig your toes into the warm white sand, you feel the lap of the ocean on your toes. *God!* With such a sigh of relief, you lean back against a palm tree. It's like everything's melting away from you, all the pain, the worry, family, heartaches, hardships—leaking out. Going down your whole body, through your legs and into the water, and letting the tide pull it out.

From the right, again out of the shadows, walks the guide. This is a shorter version. This is one you can use with the code-color word *blue*. Ask them, "What should I do about this legal case?" "What should I do about selling my house?" "What should I do about moving?" "Not moving?" "What should I do about my marriage . . ." or " . . . my relationship?" Don't get too complicated. Ask one thing at a time. And even if you don't understand what they're saying, the time will come when maybe it'll hit you right between the eyes, and say, "Oh, my God, that's what they meant. It didn't make any sense to me."

The guide comes over, sits with you, holds your hand, and more than anything, lets you know that whatever happens, they will never leave you. And at the moment of your passing, not only will your loved ones be there, but the guide will pull you through and out and take you directly to God.

Please do these exercises. They're very simplistic, and you will remember them. You can make them as elaborate as you want, as simplistic as you want. But you train your mind to get from one level to another. And the only way to do that it through meditative, active practice.

On the count of three, come up, come all the way up, feeling absolutely marvelous, better than you've ever felt before. One, two, three. . . .

ABOUT THE
SPIRIT GUIDE ARTIST
(ILLUSTRATION ON PAGE 52)

Christina Simonds's art has appeared in several books by best-selling author Sylvia Browne. Christina worked in Sylvia's office as a spiritual counselor and assistant for 10 years; was an ordained minister through Novus Spiritus; and has developed and taught spiritual classes nationwide, including Contacting Spirit Guides and Angels, utilizing her art as a visual aid.

Since her work with Sylvia, Christina has created art exclusively for Souls Enlightenment, a company she co-founded with past-life psychic medium Vera Espana (another associate of Sylvia Browne's). Together, they educate others on past-life knowledge and intuitive answers and offer spiritual art. Christina's collections include angels, goddesses, and messengers, all based on Vera's visions of the Other Side.

Christina lives in Northern California where she enjoys ongoing research for her art for Souls Enlightenment as well as giving back through the nonprofit she co-founded with Vera, Society of Enlightened Souls, to provide understanding of life's challenges through spiritual philosophy.

Website: www.selovesu.com

ABOUT THE AUTHOR

The #1 *New York Times* best-selling author **Sylvia Browne** (1936–2013) was a spiritual teacher and world-renowned psychic who appeared regularly on *The Montel Williams Show* and *Larry King Live,* and made countless other media and public appearances. With her down-to-earth personality and great sense of humor, Sylvia thrilled audiences on her lecture tours. She also wrote numerous immensely popular books, 22 of which appeared on the *New York Times* bestsellers list. Please visit www.sylviabrowne.com or call (408) 379-7070 for further information about her work.

Hay House Titles of Related Interest

YOU CAN HEAL YOUR LIFE, the movie,
starring Louise Hay & Friends
(available as a 1-DVD program, an expanded
2-DVD set, and an online streaming video)
Learn more at www.hayhouse.com/louise-movie

THE SHIFT, the movie,
starring Dr. Wayne W. Dyer
(available as a 1-DVD program, an expanded
2-DVD set, and an online streaming video)
Learn more at www.hayhouse.com/the-shift-movie

*ANIMAL SPIRIT GUIDES: An Easy-to-Use Handbook for
Identifying and Understanding Your Power Animals and
Animal Spirit Helpers* by Steven D. Farmer, Ph.D.

*ASK YOUR GUIDES: Calling in Your Divine Support System for
Help with Everything in Life* by Sonia Choquette

*DIVINE MASTERS, ANCIENT WISDOM: Activations to
Connect with Universal Spiritual Guides* by Kyle Gray

*THE SEVEN TYPES OF SPIRIT GUIDE: How
to Connect and Communicate with
Your Cosmic Helpers* by Yamile Yemoonyah

*WISDOM FROM YOUR SPIRIT GUIDES: A Handbook to
Contact Your Soul's Greatest Teachers* by James Van Praagh

All of the above are available at your local bookstore,
or may be ordered by contacting Hay House.

We hope you enjoyed this Hay House book. If you'd like to receive our online catalog featuring additional information on Hay House books and products, or if you'd like to find out more about the Hay Foundation, please contact:

Hay House, Inc., P.O. Box 5100, Carlsbad, CA 92018-5100
(760) 431-7695 or (800) 654-5126
(760) 431-6948 (fax) or (800) 650-5115 (fax)
www.hayhouse.com® • www.hayfoundation.org

———

Published in Australia by: Hay House Australia Pty. Ltd.,
18/36 Ralph St., Alexandria NSW 2015
Phone: 612-9669-4299 • *Fax:* 612-9669-4144
www.hayhouse.com.au

Published in the United Kingdom by: Hay House UK, Ltd.,
The Sixth Floor, Watson House, 54 Baker Street, London W1U 7BU
Phone: +44 (0)20 3927 7290 • *Fax:* +44 (0)20 3927 7291
www.hayhouse.co.uk

Published in India by: Hay House Publishers India,
Muskaan Complex, Plot No. 3, B-2, Vasant Kunj, New Delhi 110 070
Phone: 91-11-4176-1620 • *Fax:* 91-11-4176-1630
www.hayhouse.co.in

———

Access New Knowledge.
Anytime. Anywhere.

Learn and evolve at your own pace
with the world's leading experts.